First World War

and Army of Occupation

War Diary

France, Belgium and Germany

61 DIVISION
183 Infantry Brigade
Gloucestershire Regiment
2/6th Battalion (Territorials)
3 September 1915 - 20 February 1918

WO95/3060/2

The Naval & Military Press Ltd
www.nmarchive.com
Published in association with The National Archives

Published by

The Naval & Military Press Ltd

Unit 10 Ridgewood Industrial Park,

Uckfield, East Sussex,

TN22 5QE England

Tel: +44 (0) 1825 749494

www.naval-military-press.com

www.nmarchive.com

This diary has been reprinted in facsimile from the original. Any imperfections are inevitably reproduced and the quality may fall short of modern type and cartographic standards.

Contents

Document type	Place/Title	Date From	Date To
Miscellaneous	2/4th Bn. Gloucestershire Regiment.	01/12/1917	01/12/1917
Miscellaneous	Honours And Awards For December 1917.		
Heading	2/4th Battalion Gloucestershire Regiment Vol 21 War Diary		
War Diary	Guillaucourt	01/01/1918	04/01/1918
War Diary	Champien	08/01/1918	11/01/1918
War Diary	Voyennes	12/01/1918	13/01/1918
War Diary	Foreste	14/01/1918	18/01/1918
War Diary	Holnon Wood	19/01/1918	22/01/1918
War Diary	Fayet	26/01/1918	26/01/1918
War Diary	Holnon Wood	27/01/1918	30/01/1918
War Diary	Fayet	31/01/1918	31/01/1918
Miscellaneous	183rd Infantry Brigade.	04/01/1918	04/01/1918
Miscellaneous	2/4th Battalion Gloucestershire Regiment. Operation Order No. 107.	06/01/1918	06/01/1918
Miscellaneous	2/4th Battalion Gloucestershire Regiment. Operation Order No. 108.	10/01/1918	10/01/1918
Miscellaneous	183rd Infantry Brigade.	07/12/1917	07/12/1917
Miscellaneous	2/4th Battalion Gloucestershire Regiment. Operation Order No. 109.	12/01/1918	12/01/1918
Miscellaneous	2/4th Battalion Gloucestershire Regiment. Operation Order No. 110.	17/01/1918	17/01/1918
Miscellaneous	2/4th Battalion Gloucestershire Regiment. Operation Orders No. 111.	31/01/1918	31/01/1918
Miscellaneous	2/4th Bn Gloucester Regt. Operation Orders No.112.	23/01/1918	23/01/1918
Miscellaneous	2/4th Bn Gloucester Regt. Operation Orders No.113	24/01/1918	24/01/1918
Miscellaneous	2/4th Bn Gloucestershire Regiment.		
Heading	2/4th Bn Gloucestershire Regiment.		
War Diary	Fayet	01/02/1918	03/02/1918
War Diary	Hulnon Wood	04/02/1918	09/02/1918
War Diary	Ugny	10/02/1918	20/02/1918
War Diary	2/4th Battalion Gloucestershire Regiment. Appendix To War Diary. February 1918		
Heading	2-6 Bt. Glostershire 61 Div 183 1.B.		
Heading	2-6th Bn Glosters 1915 Sep-1918		
Heading	War Summary for August 1915		
War Diary	2/6th Battn Gloster Regt. War Diary For September 1915	02/10/1915	02/10/1915
Miscellaneous	War Summary for 1915 2/6th Battn. Gloucester Regt	02/09/1915	02/09/1915
War Diary	Epping	03/09/1915	20/09/1915
Diagram etc	Thornwood Camp Epping		
War Diary	Epping	10/10/1915	25/10/1915
War Diary	Brentwood	05/11/1915	30/11/1915
Heading	Confidential		
War Diary	White Hart Hotel Brentwood	01/12/1915	31/12/1915
Heading	Confidential		
War Diary	White Hart Hotel Brentwood	01/01/1916	31/01/1916
Miscellaneous	Operation Order No. 24. by Lieut. Colonel T.M. Carter Commanding 2/6th. Bn. Gloster Regt.,	13/01/1916	13/01/1916
Miscellaneous	2/6th. Batt. The Gloucester Regiment.	13/01/1916	13/01/1916

Miscellaneous	Tactical Exercise. on Jan 14/16th.	10/01/1916	10/01/1916
Miscellaneous	Operation Order No. 37 By Col. Sir John Barnsley V. D. Commanding	11/01/1916	11/01/1916
Operation(al) Order(s)	Operation Orders By Appendix 3	19/01/1916	19/01/1916
Miscellaneous	General Idea. Appendix 3	19/01/1916	19/01/1916
Miscellaneous	183rd Infantry Brigade. Appendix 4	27/01/1916	27/01/1916
Miscellaneous	Operation Order No. 38 Appendix 4	27/01/1916	27/01/1916
Miscellaneous	Confidential.		
War Diary	Tidworth	23/05/1916	23/05/1916
War Diary	Marguerite	24/05/1916	24/05/1916
War Diary	Havre	25/05/1916	25/05/1916
War Diary	Busnes	26/05/1916	30/05/1916
War Diary	Croix Marmuse	31/05/1916	31/05/1916
War Diary			
Heading	Confidential War Diary Vol II		
War Diary	La Cix Marmuse	01/06/1916	07/06/1916
War Diary	Richebourg St Vaast	08/06/1916	09/06/1916
War Diary	Pont du Hem	10/06/1916	10/06/1916
War Diary	Winchester House	11/06/1916	15/06/1916
War Diary	Trenches	15/06/1916	16/06/1916
War Diary	Mote D Grange Section	17/06/1916	20/06/1916
War Diary	La Gorgue	21/06/1916	28/06/1916
War Diary	Robermetz	29/06/1916	30/06/1916
War Diary	2/6th Battalion Gloster Regiment. Operation Orders No. 1 Appendix I	07/06/1916	07/06/1916
War Diary	Preliminary Order. Appendix 2	13/06/1916	13/06/1916
War Diary	Working Parties. Appendix 3		
Miscellaneous	Extract from Tactical Progress Report Appendix 3		
Miscellaneous	Tactical Progress Report Appendix 4.		
Miscellaneous	Tactical Progress Report Appendix 5		
Miscellaneous	Tactical Progress Report Appendix 6		
Miscellaneous	Battalion Routine Orders No. II		
Operation(al) Order(s)	2/6th Battalion Gloster Regiment. Operation Order No. 1 Appendix 7	20/06/1916	20/06/1916
Heading	War Diary of 2/6 Bn Gloucestershire Rgt Vol III		
War Diary	Lagorgue	01/07/1916	02/07/1916
War Diary	Laventie	03/07/1916	09/07/1916
War Diary	Trenches Nr Fauquissart	09/07/1916	19/07/1916
War Diary	Levantie	20/07/1916	31/07/1916
Miscellaneous	2/6th. Battalion Gloster Regiment. Appendix 1	03/07/1916	03/07/1916
Miscellaneous	2/6th Battalion The Gloucestershire Regiment. Appendix 2	08/07/1916	08/07/1916
Miscellaneous	183rd Brigade Order No. 23 Appendix 3		
Miscellaneous	2/6th Battalion Gloucester Regiment.	08/07/1916	08/07/1916
Miscellaneous	O.C. "C" Company Appendix 4	24/07/1916	24/07/1916
Miscellaneous	Disposition of Garrison in Post 27.7.16 Appendix 5	27/07/1916	27/07/1916
Heading	War Diary of 2/6 Bn. Gloucestershire Regt. Vol 4		
War Diary	Levantie	01/08/1916	01/08/1916
War Diary	Nr Laventie Frenches	02/08/1916	05/08/1916
War Diary	Levantie	06/08/1916	08/08/1916
War Diary	Robermetz	09/08/1916	17/08/1916
War Diary	Boutdeville	18/08/1916	18/08/1916
War Diary	Trenches Nr Neuve Chapelle	19/08/1916	22/08/1916
War Diary	Croix Barbee	23/08/1916	26/08/1916
War Diary	Trenches Nr Montes Grange	27/08/1916	31/08/1916

Miscellaneous	2/6th Battalion The Gloucestershire Regiment. Appendix I		
Miscellaneous	183rd. Brigade Order No. 33. Appendix 2		
Miscellaneous	2/6th. Battalion The Gloucestershire Regiment. Appendix 3	04/08/1916	04/08/1916
Miscellaneous	183rd. Brigade Preliminary Order. Appendix 4	07/08/1916	07/08/1916
Miscellaneous	Operation Order No. 1 Appendix 5	08/08/1916	08/08/1916
Operation(al) Order(s)	Brigade Operation Order No. 35. Appendix 6		
Miscellaneous	2/6th Battalion Gloucester Regiment Operation Orders No. 3 Appendix 7	16/08/1916	16/08/1916
Operation(al) Order(s)	2/6th. Battalion The Gloucestershire Regiment. Operation Orders No. 4 Appendix 8	17/08/1916	17/08/1916
War Diary	2/6th Battalion Gloster Regiment. Appendix 9		
Miscellaneous	2/6th Battalion Gloucester Regiment. Operation Order No. Appendix 10	25/08/1916	25/08/1916
Operation(al) Order(s)	183rd Brigade Order No. 39 Appendix II	30/08/1916	30/08/1916
Heading	War Diary of 2/6th Bn. Gloster. Regiment Vol 5		
War Diary	Trenches Riez Bailleul	01/09/1916	05/09/1916
War Diary	Moated Grange	06/09/1916	11/09/1916
War Diary	Lagorgue	12/09/1916	16/09/1916
War Diary	Neuve Chapelle	17/09/1916	20/09/1916
War Diary	Boutdeville	21/09/1916	26/09/1916
War Diary	Neuve Chapelle Sect	27/09/1916	30/09/1916
Operation(al) Order(s)	Operation Order No. 7. Appendix I	31/08/1916	31/08/1916
Miscellaneous	Operation Order No. 8 Appendix 2	05/09/1916	05/09/1916
Miscellaneous	Operation Orders No. 9 Appendix 3		
Operation(al) Order(s)	Operation Order No. 10 Appendix 4	16/09/1916	16/09/1916
Miscellaneous	Operation Orders No. 11 Appendix 5	19/09/1916	19/09/1916
Miscellaneous	Operation Order No. 11 Appendix 6	25/09/1916	25/09/1916
Heading	War Diary Of 2/6th Battalion The Gloucestershire Regiment Vol 6		
War Diary	Neuve Chapelle Sector	01/10/1916	02/10/1916
War Diary	Bout Deville	03/10/1916	08/10/1916
War Diary	Neuve Chapelle Sector	09/10/1916	14/10/1916
War Diary	Bout Deville	15/10/1916	20/10/1916
War Diary	Sector Neuve Chapelle	21/10/1916	24/10/1916
War Diary	Bout Deville	25/10/1916	26/10/1916
War Diary	Busnes	27/10/1916	31/10/1916
Operation(al) Order(s)	Operation Order No. 13 Appendix I	01/10/1916	01/10/1916
Operation(al) Order(s)	2/6th Battalion The Gloucestershire Regiment. Appendix 2	07/10/1916	07/10/1916
Operation(al) Order(s)	Operation Order No. 15 Appendix 3	09/10/1916	09/10/1916
Miscellaneous	Operation Order No. 15 Appendix 3A	13/10/1916	13/10/1916
Miscellaneous	2/6th. Battalion The Gloucestershire Regiment. Appendix 4	19/10/1916	19/10/1916
Operation(al) Order(s)	Operation Order No. 17 dated 24.10.1916 by Lt. Col. F. A. Leak Commanding 2/6th. Battn. Gloster Regt. Appendix 5	24/10/1916	24/10/1916
Operation(al) Order(s)	Operation Order No. 18 Appendix 6	26/10/1916	26/10/1916
Heading	Confidential War Diary of 2/6th Bn Gloucestershire Regt.		
War Diary	Auchel	01/11/1916	01/11/1916
War Diary	Monchy Breton	02/11/1916	02/11/1916
War Diary	Frevillers	03/11/1916	04/11/1916
War Diary	Ternas	05/11/1916	05/11/1916
War Diary	Fortel	06/11/1916	14/11/1916

War Diary	Buisberques	15/11/1916	15/11/1916
War Diary	St Leger	16/11/1916	16/11/1916
War Diary	Aveluy	17/11/1916	30/11/1916
Operation(al) Order(s)	Operation Orders No. 28 dated 29.11.1916, by Lieut. Col. F.A. Leah. Commanding 2/6th Battalion Gloucestershire Regiment. Appendix I		
Miscellaneous	War Diary. 2/6 Glosters. December 1916		
Miscellaneous	War Diary of 2/6th Battn. The Gloucestershire Regt. From Dec. 1st 1916 To Dec 31st 1916 Volume 2		
War Diary	Aveluy	01/12/1916	05/12/1916
War Diary	Trenches	06/12/1916	10/12/1916
War Diary	Martinsart Wood	11/12/1916	11/12/1916
War Diary	Varennes	12/12/1916	21/12/1916
War Diary	Martinsart Wood	22/12/1916	27/12/1916
War Diary	Trenches Nr Grandcourt	28/12/1916	31/12/1916
Heading	War Diary of 2/6th Bn. The Gloucestershire Regt. From 1.1.17 To 31.1.17 Volume 3 Vol 9		
War Diary	Warwick Huts	01/01/1917	06/01/1917
War Diary	Martinsart Wood	07/01/1917	07/01/1917
War Diary	Hedauville	08/01/1917	16/01/1917
War Diary	Raincheval	17/01/1917	17/01/1917
War Diary	Bois Bergues	18/01/1917	18/01/1917
War Diary	Prouville	19/01/1917	19/01/1917
War Diary	Argenvillers	20/01/1917	31/01/1917
Heading	War Diary of 2/6th Battn: The Gloucestershire Regt: From 1.2.17 to 28.2.17 Volume 3		
War Diary	Argenvillers	01/02/1917	04/02/1917
War Diary	Ailly Le Haut Clocher	05/02/1917	14/02/1917
War Diary	Demuin	15/02/1917	16/02/1917
War Diary	Wiencourt	17/02/1917	18/02/1917
War Diary	Framerville	19/02/1917	21/02/1917
War Diary	Trenches	22/02/1917	26/02/1917
War Diary	Framerville	27/02/1917	28/02/1917
War Diary	War Diary of 2/6 Battn The Gloucestershire Regt Vol XI		
War Diary	Framerville	01/03/1917	07/03/1917
War Diary	Trenches	08/03/1917	18/03/1917
War Diary	Brust Copse	19/03/1917	19/03/1917
War Diary	Morchain	20/03/1917	25/03/1917
War Diary	Bethencourt	26/03/1917	28/03/1917
War Diary	Monchy Legache	29/03/1917	31/03/1917
War Diary	Confidential War Diary of 2/6 Batln of Gloucestershire Regt. Vol 12		
War Diary	Monchyle Gache and Tretcon	01/04/1917	01/04/1917
War Diary	St Quentin Wood	02/04/1917	06/04/1917
War Diary	Tertry	07/04/1917	09/04/1917
War Diary	Ennemain	10/04/1917	21/04/1917
War Diary	Beauvois	22/04/1917	25/04/1917
War Diary	Vaux and Ettrelliers	26/04/1917	30/04/1917
Heading	Confidential War Diary of The 2/6th Battalion The Gloucestershire Regiment From 1.5.17 to 30.5.17 Volume 3		
War Diary	Vaux and Etreillers	01/05/1917	02/05/1917
War Diary	Trenches	03/05/1917	06/05/1917
War Diary	Holnon Wood	07/05/1917	15/05/1917
War Diary	Beauvois	16/05/1917	17/05/1917

War Diary	Nesle	18/05/1917	18/05/1917
War Diary	Coisy	19/05/1917	21/05/1917
War Diary	Beauval	22/05/1917	23/05/1917
War Diary	Grand Rullecourt	24/05/1917	24/05/1917
War Diary	Arras	25/05/1917	31/05/1917
Heading	Confidential War Diary of The 2/6th Battalion The Gloucestershire Regiment From 1.6.17 To 30.6.17 Vol 14		
War Diary	Arras	01/06/1917	01/06/1917
War Diary	Tilloy	02/06/1917	10/06/1917
War Diary	Simencourt	11/06/1917	22/06/1917
War Diary	Oeuf	23/06/1917	30/06/1917
Heading	War Diary of The 2/6th Battalion The Gloucestershire Regiment 1.7.17 to 31.7.17 Vol 15		
War Diary	Oeuf	01/07/1917	25/07/1917
War Diary	Peenhoff	26/07/1917	31/07/1917
Heading	War Diary of The 2/6th Batt The Gloucestershire Regiment From 1.8.17 to 31.8.17 Vol 1		
War Diary	Peenhoff	01/08/1917	01/08/1917
War Diary	Nr Zeggars Cappel	02/08/1917	15/08/1917
War Diary	Poperinghe	16/08/1917	16/08/1917
War Diary	Ypres	17/08/1917	17/08/1917
War Diary	Wieltje	18/08/1917	20/08/1917
War Diary	Ypres	21/08/1917	21/08/1917
War Diary	Wieltje	22/08/1917	22/08/1917
War Diary	Trenches	23/08/1917	30/08/1917
War Diary	Vlamertinghe	31/08/1917	31/08/1917
Heading	2/6 Bn Gloucestershire Regt War Diary Sept 1st 1917-Sept 30th 1917 Vol 17		
War Diary	Vlamertinghe	01/09/1917	08/09/1917
War Diary	Ypres N	09/09/1917	12/09/1917
War Diary	In Line E of Wieltse	12/09/1917	15/09/1917
War Diary	Vlamertinghe	15/09/1917	15/09/1917
War Diary	Watou Area	16/09/1917	17/09/1917
War Diary	Wormhoudt Area	18/09/1917	19/09/1917
War Diary	Simencourt	19/09/1917	23/09/1917
War Diary	Sinicholas	24/09/1917	24/09/1917
War Diary	Support Trenches	25/09/1917	30/09/1917
Heading	War Diary Oct 1-31-1917. 2/6 Gloucester Ret Vol 18		
War Diary	Trenches	01/10/1917	04/10/1917
War Diary	S Nicholas (Nr Arras)	05/10/1917	16/10/1917
War Diary	Support Trenches	17/10/1917	22/10/1917
War Diary	Front Line Trenches	23/10/1917	28/10/1917
War Diary	Support Trenches	29/10/1917	31/10/1917
Heading	2/6th Bn. The Gloucestershire Regt War Diary November 1-30 1917 Vol 19		
War Diary	In Trenches	01/11/1917	09/11/1917
War Diary	Arras	10/11/1917	21/11/1917
War Diary	In Trenches	22/11/1917	28/11/1917
War Diary	Arras	29/11/1917	30/11/1917
Heading	Confidential War Diary of 2/6 Gloucestershire Regt. From December 1st 1917 to December 31st 1917 Vol 20		
War Diary	Metz	01/12/1917	01/12/1917
War Diary	Trenches E of La Vacquerie	02/12/1917	04/12/1917
War Diary	Trenches E of La Vacquerie	05/12/1917	05/12/1917

War Diary	Havrincourt Wood	06/12/1917	10/12/1917
War Diary	Trenches E of Villers Pluich	11/12/1917	14/12/1917
War Diary	Trenches (Reserve) Beauchamp Ridek	15/12/1917	21/12/1917
War Diary	Reserve Trenches Beauchamp Ridon	22/12/1917	22/12/1917
War Diary	Havrincourt Wood	23/12/1917	23/12/1917
War Diary	Etricourt	24/12/1917	24/12/1917
War Diary	Chipilly	25/12/1917	31/12/1917
Heading	War Diary of 2/6th Battn. The Gloucester Regt Vol 21		
War Diary	Wiencourt	01/01/1918	07/01/1918
War Diary	Croiglise	08/01/1918	09/01/1918
War Diary	Falvy	10/01/1918	15/01/1918
War Diary	Ugny	16/01/1918	19/01/1918
War Diary	Trenches E of Fayet and N W of St Quentin	20/01/1918	22/01/1918
War Diary	Holnon Wood	23/01/1918	26/01/1918
War Diary	Trenches	27/01/1918	30/01/1918
War Diary	Holnon Wood	31/01/1918	31/01/1918
War Diary	St Gro 61st DW. Q	20/02/1918	20/02/1918
War Diary	Holnon Wood	01/02/1918	03/02/1918
War Diary	Vaux	04/02/1918	07/02/1918
War Diary	Guizancourt	08/02/1918	20/02/1918
Heading	2/7 Bn Worcs Reg. Sep 1915 Jan 1918		

2/4th Bn. Gloucestershire Regiment.

APPENDIX TO WAR DIARY. DECEMBER, 1917.

	Offs.	O.R.		Offs.	O.R.
EFFECTIVE STRENGTH December 1st.	33	830	December 31st.	29	555
RATION STRENGTH " "	23	638	" "	22	477

EXPLANATION OF DIFFERENCE.

	Offs.	O.R.		Offs.	O.R.
Reinforcements received	1	28	....	1	28
Casualties:-					
Killed in Action		22			
Missing	3	122			
Wounded in Action	2	90			
Evac. Sick		68			
To I.B.D. Unfit		1	....	5	303
			NET DECREASE	4	275

HONOURS AND AWARDS FOR DECEMBER 1917.

MILITARY CROSS.

Captain S.J.STOTESBURY.
Lieut. (A/Capt.) A.W.HAYWOOD.
Lieut. S.D.HARRISON.
2/Lieut. E.E.HARRIS.

DISTINGUISHED CONDUCT MEDAL.

200199 Private R. FORCE.

MILITARY MEDAL.

201652 Sergt. J.H.FOX.
202868 Corpl. S.M.SANTER.
201268 Corpl. S.HARRISON.
200238 Corpl. E.A.BOYLE.
202323 L/Cpl. B.HOOPPELL.
30587 L/Cpl. W.L.CRAMER.
235292 Pte. E.G.CLUTTERBUCK.
201080 " W.DOIDGE.
16460 " W.T.HARPER.
38306 " GARVIN J.T.
200679 " J.MEACHIN.
202241 " C.WARNES.
202299 ". W.MARTIN.
202307 " T.WITHERS.
202384 " J.SIMMONS.

BAR TO MILITARY MEDAL.

200352 Sergt. H.PORTER M.M.

------------oOo----------

2/4TH BATTALION GLOUCESTERSHIRE REGIMENT

Vol 21

WAR DIARY.

VOLUME 21.

JANUARY 1918

Instructions regarding War Diaries and Intelligence Summaries are contained in F. S. Regs., Part II. and the Staff Manual respectively. Title pages will be prepared in manuscript.

WAR DIARY
or
~~INTELLIGENCE SUMMARY~~.
(Erase heading not required.)

Army Form C. 2118.

Place	Date	Hour	Summary of Events and Information	Remarks and references to Appendices
GUILLAUCOURT	1/1/18	-	Training } Company training in morning. Individual training on Lewis Guns and Bombs in afternoon.	
"	2.1.18	-	—"—	
"	3.1.18	-	—"— Very cold frosty weather accompanied with snow.	
"	4.1.18	-	—"— During this stay at GUILLAUCOURT all O.R. in the Battn fired a Lewis Gun	
"	5.1.18	-	—"— on the range. The regular teams were also given special practice.	
"	6.1.18	-	Church Parade.	
"	7.1.18	-	Battn marched to CHAMPIEN route CAIX - QUESNEL - BOUCHOIR - ROYE (18½ miles) arrived in billets 5 p.m. Thaw set in during night 6th/7th roads very slippery in some places. Mens packs carried on lorries. The march was carried out under very difficult conditions.	
CHAMPIEN	8.1.18	-	Training Cold weather	
"	9.1.18	-	Bde: less 2/4 Glosters 2/8 Worcesters and 478 Field Coy R.E. moved to VOYENNES area. Training and baths.	
"	10.1.18	-	Training and baths.	
"	11.1.18	-	Moved to VOYENNES. Heavy rain fell during the last ¾ hour of the march. Billeting complete by 4 pm.	
VOYENNES	12.1.18	-	Training - splendid day warm sunshine.	
"	13.1.18	-	Moved to FORESTE. Move complete by 1 pm.	
FORESTE	14.1.18	-	Training.	
"	15.1.18	-	Training.	

A7092). Wt. W12839/M1297 750,000. 1/17. D. D & L., Ltd. Forms/C2118/14.

Instructions regarding War Diaries and Intelligence Summaries are contained in F. S. Regs., Part II. and the Staff Manual respectively. Title pages will be prepared in manuscript.

WAR DIARY
or
~~INTELLIGENCE SUMMARY.~~
(Erase heading not required.)

Army Form C. 2118.

Place	Date	Hour	Summary of Events and Information	Remarks and references to Appendices
FORESTE	16.1.18	–	Training Slight thaw set in.	
"	17.1.18	–	—"— Occasional showers.	
"	18.1.18	–	Presentation of ribands by G.O.C. Division. Moved to HOLNON WOOD: relieved 2/8 R. Warwicks in left Support. Battn H.Q. A C & D Coys in dugouts X 12 A. "B" Coy in dugouts M.32.d.	Nominal Roll See appendix G.
HOLNON WOOD	19.1.18	–	Quiet day, working parties	
—"—	20.1.18	–	—"— —"—	
—"—	21.1.18	–	Working parties. Weather mild. Reconnoitred forward area. Lt Col Branch went on months leave. Major Wyatt in Command.	
—"—	22.1.18	–	Major Wyatt to Bde School. Major Ross 2/7 Worcesters took over Command. Relieved 2/6 Glosters in left sub-section. Relief complete 9.45 pm. Bn H.Q. FAYET. Disposition "D" Coy Right "C" Coy Centre, "B" Coy Left, "A" Coy – Counter Attack Coy. Line held by a series of posts supported by 3 redoubts about 200x in rear of outpost line: main line of resistance (500x in rear of line of Redoubts) running N & S. through E end of village of FAYET. The trenches (recently taken over from the French) had not been revetted and had fallen in in consequence of the thaw. Movement E of line of Resistance was therefore over the open and could only be made by night.	
FAYET	23.1.18	–	Quiet day, fine mild weather	
"	24.1.18	–	—"— —"—	
"	25.1.18	–	—"— Foggy.	

A7092). Wt. W12839/M1297 750,000. 1/17. D. D & L., Ltd. Forms/C2118/14.

Army Form C. 2118.

WAR DIARY
or
~~INTELLIGENCE SUMMARY.~~
(Erase heading not required.)

Instructions regarding War Diaries and Intelligence Summaries are contained in F. S. Regs., Part II. and the Staff Manual respectively. Title pages will be prepared in manuscript.

Place	Date	Hour	Summary of Events and Information	Remarks and references to Appendices
FAYET	26.1.18	–	Quiet day, foggy. Relieved by 2/6th Glosters. relief complete 9.15 pm. Batt. moved into Left Support, taking over the same positions as before. The tour in the line was a quiet one. Our artillery was restricted to registration and counter battery work, whilst the enemy artillery showed little activity, never firing after dark. By day he fired occasional bursts at THREE COTTAGES, HOLNON and FAYET. There was a considerable amount of sniping and indirect M.G. fire on his part. Conditions were bad, trenches were impassable owing to mud and water. Casualties 1 O.R. Killed.	
HOLNON WOOD	27.1.18	–	Support – Working parties.	
–"–	28.1.18	–	–"– –"–	
–"–	29.1.18	–	–"– –"– Bathed Bn H.Q. A.C. + D Coys.	
–"–	30.1.18	–	Working party of 60 O.R. in morning. Relieved 2/6 Glosters in left sub sector of Right Sector. Relief complete without incident at 8.35 pm. Dispositions:– "B" Left "A" Centre "D" Right "C" Counter Attack. Major Hyatt resumed command.	
FAYET	31.1.18	–	Quiet day – observation very poor owing to heavy mist.	

1st February 1918.

[signature]
Major
Commanding 2/4th Glosters

A7092). Wt. W12839/M1297 750,000. 1/17. D. D & L., Ltd. Forms/C2118/14.

183rd Infantry Brigade.

Reference your S.C. 4312, of today, the undermentioned Officers, N.C.'s and men are available for decoration.

The remainder are either sick in hospital, on leave, or absent for some other reason.

MILITARY CROSS.

Capt. STOTESBURY.S.J.
A/Capt. HAYWOOD.A.W.
2/Lt. HARRIS.E.E. (Leave)

MILITARY MEDAL.

201756 Pte Monk.W.G.
235292 " Clutterbuck.E.G.
200238 Cpl Boyle.E.A.
16460 Pte Harper.W.J.* Hospital
200679 " Meachim.J.
202299 " Martin.W.
202384 " Simmons.J.
202868 Cpl Santer.S.M.
201268 " Harrison.S.
201080 Pte Doidge.W.R.
30587 L/C Cramer.W.L.
202241 Pte.Warnes.C.
202307 " Withers.T.
201682 Sergt Fox J.

Bar to MILITARY MEDAL.

200352 Sgt.Porter.H.

DIVISIONAL COMMANDER'S PARCHMENT.

202586 L/C Williams.N.

There are no men whoxare entitled to presentation who are not included on the list.

Lieut. Colonel,
4.1.18. Comdg. 2/4th Bn. Gloucestershire Regt.

2/4th Battalion Gloucestershire Regiment.

S E C R E T. [illegible] ORDER No. 1[illegible]7. Copy No. 2....

By Lieut.Colonel [illegible] [illegible] D.S.O., Commanding. In the Field, [illegible].15.

Ref. [illegible] 1/[illegible],000.

1. 2/4th Glosters will march [illegible], [illegible], [illegible].

2. [illegible]
Route:- [illegible] - [illegible] - [illegible] - [illegible].
Starting Point:- Battn.H.Q.
Order of March:- H.Q., "[illegible]", "[illegible]", "[illegible]", "[illegible]" Coys.
Head of column will pass starting point at [illegible] a.m.
Starting Point for transport:- Fork roads [illegible] [illegible]. of [illegible]
Church. Head of transport will pass starting point at [illegible] a.m.

3. [illegible] yards will be maintained between each section of six vehicles.
One Platoon of "[illegible]" Coy. will be detailed to march with and assist Transport if necessary, one section marching behind each group of six vehicles; the platoon will join transport at transport starting point and will be under orders of [illegible] Transport.

4. There will be a long halt from [illegible] p.m. until 1.[illegible] p.m. for dinners, feed and water. Water will be carried on all vehicles for watering horses. Until after the midday halt cookers will be with their companies.

5. Dress for the march:- [illegible], Haversacks worn on the back, with mess tin attached. [illegible] coats and jerkins will be placed in packs which will be carried on the lorries. Steel helmets will be strapped to the packs in the usual manner.

6. One G.S. wagon will be parked tonight at each Coy.H.Q. and one at Battn.H.Q. These will be used for carrying blankets and officers valises, mess baskets; they will be loaded by [illegible].
Packs will be dumped in company dumps at Q.M.Stores by [illegible] a.m. and will be carried on the lorries. Q.M. will send a guide to Bde.H.Q., [illegible] at [illegible] a.m. to guide lorries to Q.M. Stores.
In the event of [illegible] and the "[illegible] Precautions" coming into force special orders re transport will be issued.

7. Before leaving present area certificates that billets have been left clean will be obtained and forwarded to Battn.H.Q. as soon as possible after arrival [illegible].

8. Regimental Police will act as rearguard and march under the Orderly Officer in rear of the Battalion.

9. [illegible]

(Signed) [illegible]
Captain & Adjutant.
2/4th Battalion Gloucester Regt.

Issued at 6.30 [illegible].m.

Copies to:-

No.1. [illegible]
2 [illegible]
3-6 [illegible] Coys.
7 [illegible]
8 [illegible]
9 [illegible]
10 [illegible]
11 Spare.

[illegible]

Ref. GONNELIEU Map. (Copy).

183rd Infantry Brigade.

Herewith my report on operations of 3rd December 1917:-

At about 8.15 am. the enemy put down a very heavy barrage on the whole of the frontage held by this Battalion and attacked in very large numbers, (1) up the C.Ts. leading from CAMBRAI - GOUZEAUCOURT Road to our Front Line, (2) down our F.L. from our left flank, and (3) over the open all across our front.

Heavy casualties were inflicted by our L.G's and rifle fire on the enemy in NO MANS LAND and for a time the line held but our men were eventually forced to retire owing to very strong enemy bombing parties breaking through. Our bomb supply then became exhausted (bombing fights had been incessant during previous night and day) and the enemy advanced in very large numbers towards LA VACQUERIE. My right Coy. was practically cut off owing to enemy advancing down sunken road in 21D and a number of men are missing. Centre and left Coys. withdrew and some confusion took place in main street running N and S in 15D.
I made my way there and found that a general movement North, towards sunken road 16.a & c. was in progress. Shelling wasvery heavy. With the help of several officers I was in time to deflect a number of men and ordered them to turn left and take up a position facing East. Casualties were heavy before I could get them off the road and I found that I had a very few left by the time we had reached the open ground in 15.b. (N.of CORNER WORK). In the meantime a large number of men had gone on in the direction of the sunken road. I afterwards found that they reached a Trench at 15.b.1.6. where they came under orders of O.C.2/5th Warwicks.

My Support Coy. and Headqrs.Coy. had on the alarm being given, proceeded at once to VACQUERIE Support and adjoining trench where they put up a very good fight but were bombed out.

Cooks, Signallers, runners and sanitary men all rendered excellent service but were hopelessly outnumbered and were forced to withdraw to C.T. connecting CORNER Trench with Old British Front Line, after inflicting heavy casualties on the enemy by rifle and M.G. fire.

I instructed my Adjutant to collect all stragglers and establish themselves in O.B.F.L., touch having been obtained with 11th K.R.R. on right, time about 1.0 pm. I myself went to Battn. H.Q. of that unit (in POPE AVENUE) and reported to Brigade on telephone. I received orders from G.O.C. to send as much help as possible to O.C. 5th R.Warwicks, who, I was informed, had taken up a position in CORNER system and was in need of help. This I did and proceeded there myself but was unable to find O.C.2/5th Warwicks. I examined the position and found a number of men of the 2/5 R.Warwicks there, together with certain other details of other units.
I gave orders for fire steps to be cut and after waiting some time came across an officer, who informed me that O.C. 2/5 R.Warwicks had gone to Bde, H.Q.

I handed over command to him and returned myself to POPE AVENUE to report by phone to Bde. at about 5.0 pm.

I was informed that my men in forward posts(15.central) would be relieved by R.Berks R. and was instructed to form my Batt.H. Q. at POPE AVENUE which I did.

I wish to bring to your notice several instances of gallant conduct on the part of officers and men.

The list is now being compiled and will be forwarded by an early post.

(Signed) D.G.BARNSLEY
Lieut. Colonel,
Commanding 2/4th Gloucesters.

7.12.17

[illegible] Gloucestershire Regiment.

S E C R E T. [illegible]

By Lieut. Colonel [illegible]

Ref. Sheet [illegible]

1. The 2/4th Glosters will [illegible] 13 [illegible]

2. Method of Moving.
   Starting Point:- [illegible]
   Route:- [illegible]
   Order of March:- [illegible]
   Leading column will pass starting point at [illegible] a.m.
   There will be no [illegible] between each group of 6 vehicles. [illegible] will report to the [illegible] Officer at [illegible]

3. Blankets, officers' kits [illegible] will be [illegible] Q.M. Stores by [illegible] and [illegible] will [illegible] and 1 man to report to [illegible] at [illegible] a.m. [illegible] wagons.

4. The regimental [illegible] the Orderly Officer will act as [illegible] if necessary.

5. Billets will be left clean and a certificate [illegible] will be forwarded to the Orderly Room [illegible]

6. Falling out states and location [illegible] will be [illegible] immediately on arrival in new area.

7. Dinners will be on arrival in new area.

8. ACKNOWLEDGE.

[illegible]
Captain & Adjutant,
2/4th Bn. Gloucester Regt.

Issued at 4.30 p.m.

Copies to:-

No. 1. [illegible]
2. War Diary.
3-6 Companies.
7 [illegible]
8 [illegible]
9 [illegible]
10 183rd Inf. Bde.
11 File.

2/4th Battalion Gloucestershire Regiment.

S E C R E T. OPERATION ORDER No. 110. Copy No....2

By Lieut. Colonel D.G.BARNSLEY M.C., Commanding. In the Field.17.1.18

Reference:- 62C S.E. 1/20,000.
62B S.W. 1/20,000.

1. The 2/4th Glosters will relieve 2/8th R.Warwicks in left support on night 18/19th January.

2. "A"Coy. 2/4th Glosters will relieve "A"Coy. 2/8th R.Warwicks.
"B" " " " " " "B" " " "
"C" " " " " " "C" " " "
"D" " " " " " "D" " " "

3. Route:- Direct.
The Battalion will march off from present billets as under:-

"B"Coy.	....	3.0 p.m.
"C" "	....	3.3 p.m.
"A" "	....	3.6 p.m.
"D" "	....	3.9 p.m.
H.Q.	....	3.12 p.m.

Distances.
West of ATTILLY movement will be by companies at 200x distance.
East of ATTILLY movement will be by platoons at 200x distance.
Guides.
1 guide per platoon and 1 guide per Battalion and Coy.H.Q. will meet the Battn. at the level crossing at X.10.central.

4. Advance Party.
1 Officer per Battn.H.Q., 1 officer per Coy. and one N.C.O. per platoon will proceed to the line tomorrow morning. Guides will meet the party at X.10.central at 10.30 a.m.
Advance officers will be responsible for taking over trench stores. Lists will be carefully checked, a copy of receipts given will be sent to Battn.H.Q. by 12.0 a.m., 19th inst. Copies of receipts given for documents, maps, ~~xxxx~~, and air-photographs will be forwarded at the same time.

5. Lewis Gun limbers will proceed with companies. One water cart will accompany "B"Coy. and one will accompany Battn.H.Q. Transport Officer will arrange to have the watercarts refilled each night.
Rations will go up in limbers with the Battalion.

6. Transport Lines and Q.M.Stores will move to ETREILLERS.

7. Blankets will be rolled in bundles of 10 and will be placed in dumps inside the huts by 10.0 a.m. Each Coy. will provide a small loading party at a time to be arranged by the Transport Officer.
Officers kits and mess stores will be ready for collection by 2.0 p.m.

8. Disposition sketches showing company strength will be forwarded to Battn.H.Q. by 10.0 a.m. January 19th.

9. R.A.P. will be at Battn.H.Q. A.D.S. is near Bde.H.Q. in the sunken road at S.2.a.8.4.

10. Completion of relief will be notified by "A","C". & "D" Coys. by runner. "B"Coy. will wire relief complete - code word:- "RATIONS ARRIVED".

(Signed) S.J.STOTESBURY.
Captain & Adjutant.
2/4th Battn. Gloucester Regt.

Issued at 6.0 p.m.

Copies to:-

No.1	C.O.
2	War Diary.
3 - 6	O.C.Coys.
7	Q.M.
8	T.O.
9	M.O.M.
10	183rd Inf.Bde.
11	2/8th R. Warwicks.
12	File.

SECRET. 2/4th Battalion Gloucestershire Regiment.
OPERATION ORDER No. [illegible] Copy No. [illegible]
By Major J.D.WYATT Commanding. In the Field. [illegible]

Ref. [illegible] S.E. 1/[illegible] and S.E. 1/[illegible]

1. The 2/4 Glosters will relieve [illegible] Glosters in the Left Sub-sector of the Right Sector on night [illegible] January.
2. A Coy. 2/4 Glosters will relieve D Coy. [illegible] Glosters.
   B " " " " A " "
   C " " " " B " "
   D " " " " [illegible] " "
3. Route: HOLNON - Cross roads S.[illegible] - FAYET.
   The Battalion will move off from present billets as under:-
   B Coy. ... 5.0[illegible] C Coy. [illegible] D Coy. [illegible]
   Bn. H.Q. [illegible] A Coy. [illegible]
   Dress: Full marching order.
   Distances: All movements will be by platoons at [illegible] interval.
   Guides: 1 guide per platoon and 1 guide per Bn. & Coy.H.Q. will meet the Bn. at [illegible] S.9.[illegible]
4. Advance party: The following advance parties will proceed to the line tonight:-
   Bn. H.Q. 1 officer, 1 N.C.O., [illegible] signallers, [illegible] runners.
   Coys.H.Q. 1 officer, 1 N.C.O., 1 signaller, [illegible] runner [illegible] of Lewis Gun Teams.
   They will take with them rations for [illegible] inst. Officer i/c of each party will report to [illegible] Glosters H.Q. S.5.[illegible]9.[illegible] [illegible] guides will be obtained. Advance officers will be responsible for taking over trench stores. Lists will be carefully checked and a copy of receipt given will be forwarded to Bn. H.Q. by [illegible] inst. Copies of receipts given for documents, maps and air photographs will be forwarded at the same time.
5. Rations: Will be sent up direct to Bn. H.Q. FAYET for B, C & D Coys and Bn. H.Q. Rations for A Coy. will be taken to Coy. dump on [illegible] - FAYET road, S.[illegible]90.[illegible] O.C. A Coy. will see that a guide is posted at the dump for the information of the Transport. Companies will supply their own ration parties.
6. Water: There is one pump in FAYET which can be used for cooking and washing. The Transport officer will arrange for the two water carts to be filled and brought up each night with the rations. All dixies and petrol tins will be filled from the cart which will return to Transport Lines each night. The R.S.M. will ensure that sufficient water to supply A Coy. is left in one cart to be delivered on its return journey.
7. Lewis Guns, officers' kits and mess stores will be taken up on Coy limbers.
8. [illegible] Glosters will send the following advance parties to take over accommodation, trench stores, etc:-
   1 officer and 1 N.C.O. per Bn. and Coy. H.Q.
   1 signaller each to Bn. and [illegible] Coy. H.Q.
   Receipts for trench stores, documents, maps, etc., duly signed and countersigned by incoming units, will be rendered to this office by 12 noon 2[illegible]nd inst.
9. O.C. A Coy. will detail the following:-
   (a) 1 N.C.O. and 6 men to report to Bn. H.Q. at [illegible] [illegible] inst. They will be attached to the Regtl. Police for duty on Traffic Control Posts.
   (b) 1 complete Lewis Gun Team to be attached to D Coy. whilst the Bn. is in the line. They will report to O.C. D Coy. at [illegible] 22nd inst. for instructions.
10. Dispositions sketches showing company strengths will be forwarded to Bn. H.Q. by 10.[illegible] [illegible] inst. Sketches will show H.Q. of flanking units.
11. R.A.P. will be at Bn. H.Q.
12. Completion of relief will be notified to Bn. H.Q. Code word: "[illegible] REQUIRED".

(Sd) J.DIGBY WYATT. Major,
Commanding 2/4th Bn. Gloucestershire Regiment.

Issued at [illegible]pm.

Copy No. 1 C.O. Copy No. [illegible] War Diary. Copy No.[illegible] O.C.C.
7 Q.M. [illegible] T.O. [illegible] R.S.
10,183 Bde. 11 [illegible] Glosters. 12 File

[illegible] 2/4th Bn. Gloucester Regt Copy No....

OPERATION ORDERS No. 112.

By Major A. [illegible] Rowe, Comdg. In the field [illegible] 1-18

Ref. 62c SE 1/20,000 62b SW 1/20,000.

1. The 2/4th Glosters will be relieved by 2/6th Glos on the night [illegible] January.
After relief the Battn will move back to positions [illegible] on night 22/23rd January, Coys. taking over the same accommodation as before.

2. A Coy 2/4th Glosters will be relieved by A Coy 2/6th Glosters
B " " " " " " D " " "
C " " " " " " B " " "
D " " " " " " C " " "

3. The following guides will be sent to meet incoming unit [illegible] Bn & Coy. HQ and [illegible] per platoon (4 platoons per Coy)
B, C & D Coys guides will report at Bn. HQ. at 4.45 pm 26th inst. Guide from A Coy will be at X rds S.3.d.9.4. at 5.24 pm

4. Advance parties consisting of 1 officer and 1 N.C.O. per Bn HQ and per Coy will proceed to the new area to take over accommodation, trench stores, etc. Parties to leave the line not later than 10.0 a.m. 26th inst.
Bn HQ. and B Coy will each send in addition 1 [illegible]
Copies of receipts given for trench stores, documents, maps and air photographs will be forwarded to Bn. HQ. by 10.0 a.m. [illegible]

5 The Transport Officer will arrange to have the following [illegible] at Bn HQ. at [illegible] mess cart, water cart, 1 limber each for B C and D Coys and 1 limber for petrol tins. A Coy's limber will be sent to the company dump at [illegible] pm.
One watercart will be sent to new Bn. HQ. (T.13.a.90.70) and [illegible] to the new B Coy HQ (M.32.d.6.0.)

6 Lewis guns and equipment, Coy. stores and officers' mess [illegible] will be dumped, ready for collection by limbers, at HQ. dump, FAYET. Lewis guns will be placed under charge of senior Coy [illegible] by outgoing [illegible] after relief who will arrange for them to be loaded on Coy limber.

7. Gum boots. All gum boots will be returned to [illegible] by 12 noon 26th inst.

8. 2/6th Glosters will send the following advance parties [illegible] will take over trench stores, accommodation etc.:–
To Bn. HQ. [illegible]
To Coys 1 officer, 1 NCO and [illegible]
Receipts [illegible] trench stores, documents, maps, etc., duly [illegible] and countersigned, will be rendered to this office [illegible] 26th inst.

9. Disposition sketches showing [illegible], will be forwarded to Bn. HQ. by 10.0 a.m. 27th inst.

10. Completion of relief will be notified to Bn. HQ. Code word BRISTOL MILK.

11. ACKNOWLEDGE.

(Sgd.) E. C. S. Johnson.
Lieut. A/Adjt.
2/4th Gloucesters.

Issued at [illegible] pm

Copy No. 1	C.O.		[illegible]	R.S.M.
2	[illegible]		[illegible]	183 Bde
3-6	[illegible]		11.	2/6th Glosters
7	[illegible]		12.	File
8	[illegible]			

9th Bn Gloucester Regt

[illegible] Operation Orders No. 10

[illegible]

Ref [illegible] [illegible]

1. The [illegible] [illegible] will [illegible] [illegible] [illegible] [illegible]
[illegible] of [illegible] [illegible]
[illegible] [illegible] [illegible]

B " " " " " " [illegible]

C " " " " C " " " (Right)

[illegible] HULLMOTT [illegible] £.3.9 [illegible]

[illegible] will move off from present billets in the following order [illegible]

[illegible] pm [illegible] Rly [illegible]

[illegible] pm [illegible] Rly [illegible]

[illegible] will maintain order

[illegible] [illegible]
interval

[illegible] [illegible] will [illegible]

[illegible]

Advance parties will be detailed [illegible]

Bn HQ [illegible] officer, [illegible] 2 [illegible]

Coy [illegible] officer, [illegible] 1 [illegible]

Party from [illegible] will proceed [illegible] the [illegible]
[illegible] tomorrow morning. Officer [illegible]
will report [illegible] HQ [illegible] where [illegible]
will be obtained. Advance officers will be responsible for
taking over [illegible] huts will [illegible] checked
and a copy [illegible] will be forwarded to Bn HQ
by 10 am [illegible] with [illegible] given
for documents [illegible] are [illegible]

[illegible]

[illegible] Rations for [illegible] will [illegible]
[illegible] will [illegible] rations parties

[illegible] Officer will [illegible]
[illegible] brought up each night [illegible]
[illegible], [illegible]
[illegible] will be taken up [illegible] Coy [illegible]
[illegible]

The Transport Officer will arrange for the [illegible]
[illegible] at [illegible] 4.45 [illegible]
[illegible] for A Coy [illegible] for Bn HQ [illegible]
[illegible]
[illegible] at 50 [illegible]
[illegible]

[illegible] parties [illegible]
[illegible]

[illegible]

[illegible]

[illegible]
[illegible]

C Coy will [illegible] the following:-

(a) 1 N.C.O. and 3 men to report [illegible] inst. for duty on Traffic [illegible]

(b) 1 complete L.G. team [illegible] whilst the Bn is in the line [illegible] to O.C. D Coy at 4.15pm 30th inst. for [illegible]

(c) 1 platoon to be attached to B Coy whilst the Bn is in the line – to report to O.C. B Coy at [illegible] 30th inst.

Disposition sketches showing [illegible] strengths will be forwarded to Bn. H.Q. by 10 a.m. 31st inst. Sketches to show H.Q. of flanking units.

Gum boots will be taken over by Bn. H.Q. at [illegible] Boot Store.

Pass word to be used by all patrols whilst the [illegible] in the line "RED TRIANGLES". O.C. B and [illegible] Coys will advise Battn on plans.

Completion of relief will be notified to [illegible] Code word:- "JERUSALEM".

5 ACKNOWLEDGE.

(Sd) E. C. S. [illegible]
Lieut. [illegible]
2/4th [illegible]

Issued at 6.0 pm.

Copy No 1. C.O.
2. War Diary.
3-6 O.C. Coys.
7 QM
8 T.O.
9 R.S.M.
10. 183 Inf. Bde.
11. 2/6 Glosters
12. File

2/4th Bn Gloucestershire Regiment.

APPENDIX TO WAR DIARY. JANUARY 1918.

		Offs.	O.R.		Offs.	O.R.
EFFECTIVE STRENGTH.	Jnuary 1st	29.	555.	January 31st	43.	622.
RATION STRENGTH	" "	22.	477.	" "	34.	561.

	Offs.	O.R.
REINFORCEMENTS RECEIVED................................	16.	122.

DECREASE.	Offs.	O.R.
EVAC.SICK.		25.
TO ENGLAND SICK	1.	18.
TFD. L.T.M.B.	1.	2.
To I.B.D. UNFIT.		8.
DIED OF WOUNDS.		1.
TFD. Div.H.Q.,		1.

	Offs.	O.R.
	2.	55.
NET INCREASE.	14.	67

2/4th BATTALION GLOUCESTERSHIRE REGIMENT.

16

183/61

WAR DIARY.

VOLUME. 22.

FEBRUARY 1918.

Instructions regarding War Diaries and Intelligence Summaries are contained in F. S. Regs., Part II. and the Staff Manual respectively. Title pages will be prepared in manuscript.

WAR DIARY

or

INTELLIGENCE SUMMARY.

(Erase heading not required.)

Army Form C. 2118.

Place	Date	Hour	Summary of Events and Information	Remarks and references to Appendices
[illegible]	[illegible]		[illegible]	
	[illegible]		[illegible] A D B	
	[illegible]		[illegible] E HOLNON WOOD	
HOLNON WOOD	[illegible]		[illegible]	
	[illegible]		[illegible]	
	[illegible]		[illegible]	
	[illegible]		Working Parties	
	[illegible]		Working Parties	
	[illegible]		[illegible]	
[illegible]	[illegible]		[illegible]	

A7092). Wt. W12839/M1297 750,000. 1/17. D. D & L., Ltd. Forms/C2118/14.

Instructions regarding War Diaries and Intelligence Summaries are contained in F. S. Regs., Part II. and the Staff Manual respectively. Title pages will be prepared in manuscript.

WAR DIARY
or
~~INTELLIGENCE~~ SUMMARY.

(Erase heading not required.)

Army Form C. 2118.

Place	Date	Hour	Summary of Events and Information	Remarks and references to Appendices
UGNY	12/4/18	-	Working Parties on gun emplacements on BEAUVOIS HAM Road	
	13/4/18	-		
	14/4/18	-		
	15/4/18	-		
	16/4/18	-		
	17/4/18	-		
	18/4/18	-		
	19/4/18	-		
	20/4/18		Moved to [illegible] to concentrate as a portion of No 24 Entrenching Battn. A portion of W.O's and N.C.O's returned to No 55 I B D. Surplus personnel of 2/6th GLOSTERS, 4/7 WORCESTERS and 7/5th R WARWICKS joined us	

A7092). Wt. W128:9/M129? 750,000. 1/17. D. D & L., Ltd. Forms/C2118/14.

2/4th Battalion Gloucestershire Regiment.

APPENDIX TO WAR DIARY. FEBRUARY 1918.

	Offs.	O.R.	Offs.	O.R.
EFFECTIVE STRENGTH. FEBRUARY 1st.	43.	608.		
RATION STRENGTH. " "	29.	51[illegible].		

	Offs.	O.R.
REINFORCEMENTS RECEIVED..............................	3.	15.

DECREASE

	Offs.	O.R.
EVAC. SICK.	-	35.
TO ENGLAND SICK.	[illegible].	[illegible].
TFD. TO BASE DEPOT AS REINFORCEMENTS.		6.
TO ENGLAND FOR COMMISSION.		1.
TFD TO VTH ARMY SCHOOL.		1.
STRUCK OFF STRENGTH UNDER G.R.O.3396		1.
DIED OF SICKNESS.		1.
TFD. TO 267 M.G. COY.		4.
TFD TO 2/5th GLOUCESTERS.	16.	20[illegible].
TRANSPORT ATTD TO 51st DIVISION.	1.	34.

REMAINDER OF PERSONNEL OF 2/4th Glboucesters were posted to No.24 Entrenching Battalion as and from 21st inst.

2 - 6 BT. GLOSTERSHIRE

61 DIV.

183 I. B.

61ST DIVISION
183RD INFY BDE

2-6TH BN GLOSTERS

~~MAY 1916 - FEB 1918~~

1915 SEP — ~~1916 JAN~~

~~1916 MAY~~ — 1918 FEB

(1916 FEB, MAR, APR, DIARIES MISSING)

DISBANDED

War Summary for August 1915

Unit – 2/6th Battn Gloster Regt.

Brigade 183rd Infantry Brigade

Division 61st Division.

Mobilization Centre – Bristol

Concentration centre Northampton

Stations since occupied

Epping
Chelmsford
Kelvedon
Danbury.
Epping.

Thos M Carter
Lt Col
O.C. 2/6th Bn Gloster Regt.

2/6th Battn Gloster Regt.

War Diary for September 1915

Epping. Oct 2. 1915

Unit. 2nd 6th Battn Gloster Regt.

Brigade 183rd Infantry Brigade

Division 61st (South Midland) Division

Mobilization Centre — Bristol

Concentration Centre Northampton

Stations subsequently occupied

Epping
Chelmsford
Kelvedon
Danbury
Epping

Thos. W. Carter.
Col.

War Summary for 1915

2/6th Battn Gloucester Regt

EPPING Septr 2. 1915.

d. During the month much attention has been given to Entrenchments and considerable experience gained in planning and digging trenches. A useful exercise was afforded during the last week of the month by the occupation of trenches at MALDON (constructed by the 2/7th Battn Worcester Regt) by each company for 24 hours.
Field training has been difficult to carry out satisfactorily on account of the few men available for duty.

Thos M Carter
Lt Col.

2/6th Battn Glosters Regt.

Instructions regarding War Diaries and Intelligence Summaries are contained in F. S. Regs., Part II. and the Staff Manual respectively. Title pages will be prepared in manuscript.

WAR DIARY *or* ~~INTELLIGENCE SUMMARY.~~ for September 1915

(Erase heading not required.)

Army Form C. 2118.

Place	Date	Hour	Summary of Events and Information	Remarks and references to Appendices
Epping	3rd		24 men transferred from 82nd Provisional Battalion	
	6th		11 men sent from 3/6th Battn Glosters Regt (to replace 11 of previous Draft found medically unfit)	
	12th		at 11·50 last night (11/12/9/15) a Zeppelin passed over camp dropping a large number of incendiary and six H.E Bombs No one was injured and no damage done. The H.E. bombs failed to explode and sunk from 7 to 8 feet into the clayey soil. Officers of 2/8 Bn Worc Regt saw the airship travelling northwards at about 11·45 over their Camp (which lies due S of this one) and 2 officers of this Battn saw it travelling rapidly northwards from the West Corner of this camp. I myself was awakened at 11·50 & heard bombs falling & saw lurid glare to N of my tent. Seven incendiary bombs were blazing harmlessly in the field immediately N of the Officers lines and further fires were blazing N.W of the Camp. At daylight six H.E. bombs were found buried deep in the ground [illegible]	
	13		Capt O. Davis R.E. visited Camp and gave instructions for H.E. bombs to be dug out. 33 Incendiary Bombs (No 4 pattern) have been found by Police & military.	
	14		Six bombs removed. Spherical No 2 pattern. Fuses removed by Capt Davis but all fired at 6 pm one bomb was fired in a pit with a light guncotton charge, it was broken open but failed to detonate. Another H.E bomb found in ditch at road junction E of Camp: in the loose soil it was buried only about 3 feet.	

1577 Wt. W10791/1773 500,000 1/15 D. D. & L. A.D.S.S./Forms/C. 2118.

2/6th Bn Gloster Regt

Instructions regarding War Diaries and Intelligence Summaries are contained in F. S. Regs., Part II. and the Staff Manual respectively. Title pages will be prepared in manuscript.

WAR DIARY for September 1915 (Continued)
or
INTELLIGENCE SUMMARY.
(Erase heading not required.)

Army Form C. 2118.

Place	Date	Hour	Summary of Events and Information	Remarks and references to Appendices
Epping				
	15		Another H.E. bomb found in field E of Camp.	
			Unexploded Incendiary bomb found (isolated from all others) in hedge 300 yds N of Camp.	
	17		2 N.C.O's + 8 men transferred to 82nd Provisional Battalion on medical grounds.	
	20		3 men discharged as no longer physically fit for war service.	
			Note — The accompanying sketch map of the situation of Bombs represents the probable course of the Airship – throwing 4 H.E. bombs on each side.	
			The map has been drawn by 2nd Lieut C.S. Lewis.	

Thos. McCarter Lt Col
2/6th Bn Gloster Regt

1577 Wt. W10791/1773 500,000 1/15 D. D. & L. A.D.S.S./Forms/C. 2118.

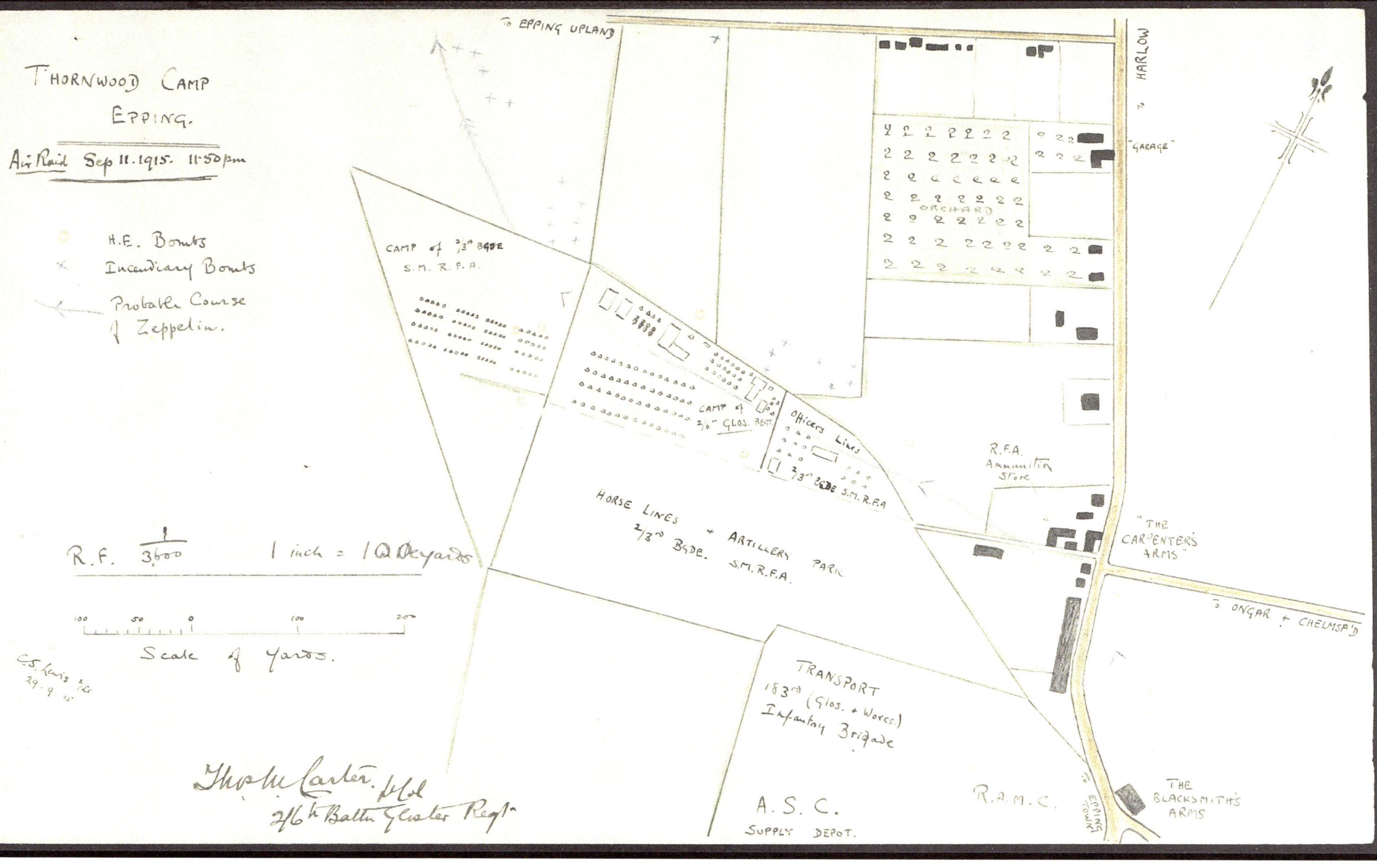

Thornwood Camp
Epping.
Air Raid Sep 11. 1915. 11·50pm
H.E. Bombs
Incendiary Bombs
Probable Course of Zeppelin.
To Epping Upland
To Harlow
"Garage"
Orchard
Camp of 2/3rd Bgde S.M. R.F.A.
Camp of 2/6th Glos. Regt.
Officers Lines
2/3rd Bgde S.M. R.F.A
R.F.A. Ammunition Store
Horse Lines + Artillery Park 2/3rd Bgde. S.M.R.F.A.
"The Carpenters Arms"
To Ongar + Chelmsf'd
Transport 183rd (Glos. + Worcs.) Infantry Brigade
A. S. C. Supply Depot.
R.A.M.C.
To Epping Town
The Blacksmiths Arms
R.F. 1/3600
1 inch = 100 yards
100 50 0 100 200
Scale of Yards.
C.S. Lewis 2/Lt 29.9.15.
Thos M Carter. Lt Col
2/6th Battn Gloster Regt

Instructions regarding War Diaries and Intelligence Summaries are contained in F. S. Regs., Part II. and the Staff Manual respectively. Title pages will be prepared in manuscript.

2/6th Bn Gloster Regt

WAR DIARY *or* INTELLIGENCE SUMMARY. for October 1915.

(*Erase heading not required.*)

Army Form C. 2118.

Place	Date	Hour	Summary of Events and Information	Remarks and references to Appendices
EPPING	10/10/15		2nd Lieut. L. W. Just joined for duty.	
	18/10/15		Lieut Herbert Smith (RAMC.T) joined for duty. Capt RJ Moore (RAMC.T) transferred to 2/2 S.M.F.A.	
	25/10/15		Moved station (under Brigade arrangements) to BRENTWOOD.	

Thos M Carter Lt Col

1577 Wt. W10791/1773 500,000 1/15 D. D. & L. A.D.S.S./Forms/C. 2118.

CONFIDENTIAL

3/6th Bn Gloster Regt

WAR DIARY
or
~~INTELLIGENCE SUMMARY~~.
(Erase heading not required.)

for November (1914) 1915

Army Form C. 2118.

Instructions regarding War Diaries and Intelligence Summaries are contained in F. S. Regs., Part II. and the Staff Manual respectively. Title pages will be prepared in manuscript.

Place	Date	Hour	Summary of Events and Information	Remarks and references to Appendices
BRENTWOOD	5/11/15		2 Officers, 19 NCO's & men, accompanied by the Band returned to Bristol on a recruiting tour.	
	23/11/15		3 NCO's & 16 men (Home Service Bandsmen) transferred to Administrative Centre	
	30/11/15		13 Officers transferred to 3/6th Bn Gloster Regt at Cheltenham.	

Theo. W. Carter
Lt Col

1577 Wt. W10791/1773 500,000 1/15 D. D. & L. A.D.S.S./Forms/C. 2118.

C O N F I D E N T I A L.

War Diary of

2nd 6th. Battalion., Glos. Regimant.

from 1st. December, 1915, to 31st. December 1915.

Volume 2.

Army Form C. 2118.

Instructions regarding War Diaries and Intelligence Summaries are contained in F. S. Regs., Part II. and the Staff Manual respectively. Title pages will be prepared in manuscript.

WAR DIARY
or
~~INTELLIGENCE SUMMARY.~~
(Erase heading not required.)

Place	Date	Hour	Summary of Events and Information	Remarks and references to Appendices
White Hart Hotel Brentwood	1.12.15	6.30 pm.	Company Training	[illegible]
— do —	2.12.15	-do-	Battalion paraded 8.45 under Capt Rudman & proceeded to MOUNTNESSING for the purpose of digging trenches on the LONDON defences.	
			Institute opened in Town Hall, facilities provided for writing, weekly papers etc	[illegible]
— do —	3.12.15	-do-	Company training	
			Inspection of B.N. 1st Line Transport by the Commanding Officer.	[illegible]
— do —	4.12.15	-do-	Battalion parade 9.30 Route March	
			2nd Lt C.S. Lewis appointed officer in Charge of Scouts vice 2nd Lt G.F. Briggs	[illegible]
			Horse No 7718 taken on the Strength.	
— do —	5.12.15	-do-	Church Parades.	[illegible]
— do —	6.12.15	-do-	Company training	[illegible]
— do —	7.12.15	-do-	Battalion Paraded 8.45 & proceeded to MOUNTNESSING for the purpose	[illegible]
— do —			of digging trenches on the London defences.	
— do —	8.12.15	-do-	Company Training	[illegible]
— do —	9.12.15	-do-	Company Training.	
			Received authority to transfer 9 men to 82nd Provisional Batt. Authority o/c T.F. Records Warwick reference P1725 dated 3.12.15.	[illegible]

1577 Wt. W10791/1773 500,000 1/15 D. D. & L. A.D.S.S./Forms/C. 2118.

Sheet (2)

Instructions regarding War Diaries and Intelligence Summaries are contained in F. S. Regs., Part II. and the Staff Manual respectively. Title pages will be prepared in manuscript.

WAR DIARY
or
~~INTELLIGENCE SUMMARY.~~
(Erase heading not required.)

Army Form C. 2118.

Place	Date	Hour	Summary of Events and Information	Remarks and references to Appendices
White Hart Hotel Brentwood	9.12.15	6.30 pm.	The undermentioned officers, N.C.Os, proceeded to WITHAM for a course of Instruction in the use of hand grenades. Lieut Eyre, 2nd Lieut Cavell, 2nd Lieut Gardner, 3863 a/Cpl Brunt 3515 a/Serjt Straker, 1581 a/Serjt Jones The following appeared in London Gazette. Lieuts to be Temporary Captains R.W.G. Cox (Nov: 15th) P.H.H. Beck (Nov: 17th) 2nd Lieuts to be Temporary Lieuts H.W. Eyre (Nov: 20th).	RAY
-do-	10.12.15	-do-	Company Training	RAY
-do-	11.12.15	-do-	Battalion Parade 9.30 a.m Route March (full marching order) 10 miles	RAY.
-do-	12.12.15	-do-	Church Parades.	RAY.
-do-	13.12.15	-do-	Company Training. Capt Stronge-Ikarn sat as a member of District Court Martial, Capt P.H.H. Beck & Lieut H.W. Eyre attended for instruction.	RAY.
-do-	14.12.15	-do-	Company Training	RAY.

1577 Wt. W10791/1773 500,000 1/15 D. D. & L. A.D.S.S./Forms/C. 2118.

Shut (3)

Instructions regarding War Diaries and Intelligence Summaries are contained in F. S. Regs., Part II. and the Staff Manual respectively. Title pages will be prepared in manuscript.

WAR DIARY
~~or~~
~~INTELLIGENCE SUMMARY.~~

(Erase heading not required.)

Army Form C. 2118.

Place	Date	Hour	Summary of Events and Information	Remarks and references to Appendices
White Hart Hotel Brentwood	15.12.15	6.30 pm	Battalion paraded at 9.30 a.m & proceeded to Mountnessing for instruction in Sand bag revetments	
			Received certificate that 2nd Lieut L. W. Just passed "Excellent" in both pratical & theoretical at his course of Instruction in Infantry Pioneering at Ongar Nov 29th to Nov: 29th	RAJ
—do—	16.12.15	—do—	Company Training	RAJ
	17.12.15		—do—	
			Four Recruits taken on the strength, having arrived from Bristol	RAJ
	18.12.15	—do—	Brigade Route March. Route BRENTWOOD, EAST HORNDON – MONKS – GREAT WARLEY STREET to BRENTWOOD distance about 12 miles [illegible]	RAJ
	19.12.15	—do—	Church Parades	RAJ
	20.12.15	—do—	Company Training in the Morning.	RAJ
			Battalion Night March	RAJ
	21.12.15	—do—	Company Training	
			Inspection by Col. Collis A.S.C. of 1st line Transport	
			Recruit 4494 Pte H. J. Fay having arrived from Bristol is taken on the strength	RAJ

1577 Wt. W10791/1773 500,000 1/15 D. D. & L. A.D.S.S./Forms/C. 2118.

Sheet (4)

Instructions regarding War Diaries and Intelligence Summaries are contained in F. S. Regs., Part II. and the Staff Manual respectively. Title pages will be prepared in manuscript.

WAR DIARY

~~or~~

~~INTELLIGENCE SUMMARY.~~

(Erase heading not required.)

Army Form C. 2118.

Place	Date	Hour	Summary of Events and Information	Remarks and references to Appendices
White Hart Hotel Brentwood.	21.12.15	6.30 p.m	2nd Lieut Calvert-Fisher, 3131 a/cpl A. W. Patterson & No 2863 a/cpl J. A. Brunt proceeded to Kelvedon for a Course of Instruction in Trench fighting.	
			Regimental Course (machine Gun) commenced	RAY
	22.12.15.		Company Training	RAY.
	23.12.15.		Company Training in the Morning	
			Battalion parade 3.30 p.m for Night outpost scheme	
	24.12.15		Company training.	
			Major General R Bannatine-Allason visited the Battalion.	
	25.12.15		Church Parades	
			No 3892 ~~Private~~ E J Yates died on the night of 24/25th from natural causes.	
	26.12.15.		Church Parades.	
	27.12.15.		Company training.	
			No 3980 Pte R.C. Bennett having arrived at this station from 3/6 Glos Regt Cheltenham has been taken on the Strength & posted to "C" Coy (married)	RAY.
			~~The following officers have been granted leave Lieut H Smith (RAMC T.)~~	

1577 Wt. W10791/1773 500,000 1/15 D. D. & L. A.D.S.S./Forms/C. 2118.

Sheet V

Instructions regarding War Diaries and Intelligence Summaries are contained in F. S. Regs., Part II. and the Staff Manual respectively. Title pages will be prepared in manuscript.

WAR DIARY

~~or~~

~~INTELLIGENCE SUMMARY.~~

(Erase heading not required.)

Army Form C. 2118.

Place	Date	Hour	Summary of Events and Information	Remarks and references to Appendices
White Hart Hotel Brentwood	28.12.15	6.30 p.m.	Company training in the morning. Battalion Parade 4.30 p.m. Night March (12 miles)	RAY.
	29.12.15	-do-	Company training Regimental Course of Range-Finding Commenced Arrangements made for a Monthly Prize for Cooking to commence Jan 1st 1916. Received Certificates for Courses attended by 2nd Lieuts A. W. Trotman & L. W. Just at the Course of Instruction Cambridge from Nov 22nd to Dec 21st & at Chelsea from Dec: 13th to Dec 24th respectively Lieut Col. B. F. B. Stuart C.B. attached to the Brigade for duty.	RAY RAY
	30.12.15	-do-	Company training	
	31.12.15	9.30 a.m.	Company training in the Morning. Battalion Parade 4.30 p.m. with 1st Line transport for Night March.	RAY

Thos M. Carter Lt Col

O.C. 2/6th Batt. Gloster Regt.

1577 Wt. W10791/1773 500,000 1/15 D. D. & L. A.D.S.S./Forms/C. 2118.

C O N F I D E N T I A L .

WAR DIARY OF

2/6th.Battalion The Gloucester Regiment.

from 1st. ~~December~~ January ~~1915~~ 1916 to 31st. ~~December~~ January ~~1915~~ 1916.

January 1916

Instructions regarding War Diaries and Intelligence Summaries are contained in F. S. Regs., Part II. and the Staff Manual respectively. Title pages will be prepared in manuscript.

WAR DIARY

or

~~INTELLIGENCE SUMMARY.~~

(Erase heading not required.)

Army Form C. 2118.

Page 1

Place	Date	Hour	Summary of Events and Information	Remarks and references to Appendices
WHITE HART HOTEL BRENTWOOD.	1.1.16	6.30pm	Battalion Parade 9.30 a m Route March	
			Col. Sir JOHN BARNSLEY V.D. having proceeded on leave Col. A.G. PEYTON 8/7 [illegible] assumes Command of the Brigade.	RAY
	2.1.16.	5pm	Church Parades	
			Col Sir JOHN BARNSLEY V.D. having returned from leave assumes Command of the Brigade.	RAY
	3.1.16	7pm	Company training.	
			Sentence of D.C.M on Pte PORTER (91 days detention) Promulgated.	
			Col Sir JOHN. BARNSLEY V.D. having proceeded overseas to-day Lieut Col. [illegible] assumes Command of the Brigade.	
			No 4226 Pte G.S. NORA A Coy having been declared illegally absent since Dec 11th 1915 is struck off the Strength from that date	
			Recruits Nos 4996 J DUVAL & No 4998 [illegible] having arrived at this station are taken on the strength.	RAY

1577 Wt. W10791/1773 500,000 1/15 D. D. & L. A.D.S.S./Forms/C. 2118.

Instructions regarding War Diaries and Intelligence Summaries are contained in F. S. Regs., Part II. and the Staff Manual respectively. Title pages will be prepared in manuscript.

~~WAR~~ DIARY
~~or~~
~~INTELLIGENCE SUMMARY.~~
(Erase heading not required.)

Army Form C. 2118.

Page 2

Place	Date	Hour	Summary of Events and Information	Remarks and references to Appendices
WHITE HART HOTEL BRENTWOOD.	4.1.16	5:30pm	Battalion parade 9.30 a.m. Route march full marching order route BRENTWOOD – BROOK-STREET TYLERS-COMMON UPMINSTER RECTORY BELES GREAT-WARLEY STREET WARLEY HARTS WOOD BRENTWOOD Ref 1" OS Sheet 108, distance about 12 miles	RAJ
	5.1.16	6:30pm	Company training Monthly inspection of ammunition by the Commanding Officer Companies instructed in mess tin cooking night march 1st line transport (4.30 p.m – 7.30 p.m)	RAJ
	6.1.16.	7pm	Sandbag revetments.	
	7.1.16.	5.pm.	Company training (9.30 – 12.30 a.m). 2.30pm Lecture in Town Hall by M.O. on Military Hygiene & First Field dressings	RAJ
	8.1.16	5.30pm.	Battalion Parade 9.30 am. Route March, full marching order. Route BRENTWOOD – BROOK STREET – HARE STREET – SQUIRRELS HEATH – HAROLD WOOD – BROOK STREET – BRENTWOOD 1" OS Sheet 108. distance about 12 miles LT-COL. T.M. CARTER having proceeded on leave CAPT. F.J LANGFORD assumed temporary Command.	RL

T2134. Wt. W708–776. 500000. 4/15. Sir J. C. & S.

Instructions regarding War Diaries and Intelligence Summaries are contained in F. S. Regs., Part II. and the Staff Manual respectively. Title pages will be prepared in manuscript.

WAR DIARY

~~or~~

~~INTELLIGENCE SUMMARY.~~

(*Erase heading not required.*)

Army Form C. 2118.

Place	Date	Hour	Summary of Events and Information	Remarks and references to Appendices
WHITE HART HOTEL BRENTWOOD.	8.1.16	5.30pm	CAPT R A YOUNG having proceeded on leave of absence LIEUT R LOWTHER acting Adjutant.	
			COL SIR JOHN BARNSLEY having returned from overseas resumes command of the Brigade.	RL
	9.1.16	6.30pm	Church Parades.	RL
	10.1.16	8.40pm	9.30–11. Battalion Close order Drill.	
			Battalion Parade 4.30 – 8.30 p.m. Route March Route BRENTWOOD – SHENFIELD – PALMERS	
			FARM – PILGRIMS HATCH – SOUTH WEALD – BROOKSTREET – BRENTWOOD.	
			Ref O.S. 1" Sheet 108 Distance about 11 miles	RL
	11.1.16	6.30pm	Battalion parade Close order drill 9.30 10.30 a.m	
			Company training 10.30 – 12.30 2.30 – 4.30	
			LT. COL T M CARTER having returned from leave resumes command of the Battalion.	RL
	12.1.16	6.30pm	Company training	RL
	13.1.16	7pm	Battalion parade for Regimental Exercise 9.30 – 4.30 p.m	Appendix 1 RL
	14.1.16	6.30pm	Brigade Exercise, the Battalion was in reserve at BILLERICAY	Appendix 2 RL
	15.1.16	7pm	Company training.	RL

T2134. Wt. W708–776. 500000. 4/15. Sir J. C. & S.

Army Form C. 2118.

WAR DIARY ~~or~~ ~~INTELLIGENCE~~ SUMMARY.

(*Erase heading not required.*)

Instructions regarding War Diaries and Intelligence Summaries are contained in F. S. Regs., Part II. and the Staff Manual respectively. Title pages will be prepared in manuscript.

Page 4

Place	Date	Hour	Summary of Events and Information	Remarks and references to Appendices
WHITE HART HOTEL BRENTWOOD.	16/1/16	10.30pm	Church Parades	
			Wire received from O/C 3/6th Glosters stating draft of 280 men arriving this station 17/1/16	RL
	17/1/16	9.0pm	CAPT R.A. YOUNG returned from leave of absence.	
			Owing to shortage of billets, we decided to billet 5 officers & 170 N.C.O's & men at ~~Shenfield~~, ~~[illegible]~~ SHENFIELD. This was carried out by 4.30pm.	
			Draft of 275 men arrived from 3/6th Glosters at 7.0pm after a wire had been received stating 5 men of 280 detailed to report were absentees.	RAY.
	18/1/16	6.0pm	Company training	
			Draft formed into a Recruit Company under LIEUT. LOWTHER.	
			Medical examination of draft commenced.	RAY
	19/1/16	9.30pm	Company Training 9.30 - 12.0 noon.	
			2 Squads, - one in Bayonet Fighting & 1 in Physical Training were inspected by the District Inspecting Supervisor of Gymnasia	~~RAY~~
			The Battalion paraded at 6.0pm for night exercise	Appendix 3 RAY.

T.2134. Wt. W708—776. 500000. 4/15. Sir J. C. & S.

Instructions regarding War Diaries and Intelligence Summaries are contained in F. S. Regs., Part II. and the Staff Manual respectively. Title pages will be prepared in manuscript.

WAR DIARY
or
~~INTELLIGENCE SUMMARY~~.
(Erase heading not required.)

Army Form C. 2118.

Page 5

Place	Date	Hour	Summary of Events and Information	Remarks and references to Appendices
WHITE HART	20/1/16	9.45pm	Inspection by MAJOR GENERAL E.T. DIXON Inspector of Infantry	
HOTEL			Received orders as to the discontinuance of the use of the [illegible]	R.A.Y.
BRENTWOOD	21/1/16	6.30pm	~~Company Training~~	
	22/1/16	2pm	Battalion Exercise Route - BRENTWOOD - SHENFIELD - PT 175 - WOODLANDS - to PT 213. when the Battn halted & the officers went forward to view the ground, with the intent of attacking the enemy who have been reported to be holding the village of DODDINGHURST the Battalion returned to Billets via PETTITS FARM - PT 219 - GALLOWS GREEN Ref O.S. Sheet No 1" [illegible]	R.A.Y.
	23.1.16	7.30pm	Church Parades.	R.A.Y.
	24/1/16	6.30pm	Commenced digging short lengths of trenches at varying distances from one another for practising accuracy of throwing hand grenades	
			Regimental Course of Range finding Commenced - 8 N.C.O's & 2 privates.	R.A.Y.
	25/1/16		Maj General R. BANNATINE - ALLISON C.B inspected the recruits of the unit	
			Col: Sir JOHN BARNSLEY V.D & Col. A.G. PAYTON gave a lecture on their recent visit to the B.E.F. France	R.A.Y.

Instructions regarding War Diaries and Intelligence Summaries are contained in F. S. Regs., Part II. and the Staff Manual respectively. Title pages will be prepared in manuscript.

WAR DIARY

~~or~~

~~INTELLIGENCE SUMMARY.~~

(*Erase heading not required.*)

Army Form C. 2118.

Page 6

Place	Date	Hour	Summary of Events and Information	Remarks and references to Appendices
WHITE HART HOTEL BRENTWOOD.	26.1.16	7 p.m	Company training	~~op~~ RAY.
	27.1.16	8.30 pm	Brigade Exercise	appendix 4 RAY
	28.1.16	6 pm	Company training	
			Received a certificate that 2nd Lt E.N GARDNER qualified as a Brigade Instructor in Bombing at GODSTONE Jan 2nd to 15th 1916.	RAY
	29.1.16	8 p.m.	Company training.	
			The following appeared in the LONDON GAZETTE.	
			CAPTAIN F J. LANGFORD to be temp MAJOR Jan 1st 1916 also CAPTAIN G STRONGITHARM Jan 8th 1916.	
			LIEUT R LOWTHER to be temp CAPTAIN Jan 8th 1916 also LIEUT ~~[illegible]~~ H.W. EYRE dated Jan 11th 1916.	
			Received a satisfactory certificate for 2nd Lt S.E.B. SAGE for his course of instruction 3rd ARMY TRENCH FIGHTING SCHOOL KELVEDON from DEC 8th to 18th 1915.	RAY.
	30.1.16	7 pm	Church Parades.	RAY.
	31.1.16	6 pm	Company training.	RAY.

Thos M Carter.
LIEUT COLONEL
COMMANDING 2/6 Glos: Regt

T2134. Wt. W708—776. 500000. 4/15. Sir J. C. & S.

Appendix 1.

OPERATION ORDER No.24.

by

Lieut.Colonel T.M.Carter

COMMANDING 2/6th.Bn.Gloster Regt.,

Copy No.

Brentwood. 13.1.1916. 5a.m.

Ref. ½" O.S. Sheet 29.

1.We have obtained possession of the Railway (Great Eastern Main line) and occupied BRENTWOOD and ROMFORD.

2/6th.Bn.Gloster Regiment. 2.The force as per margin is ordered to be at HAVERING - ATTE - BOWER at 12noon to-day and to take up position N.W. of that place.

Scouts. 3.The Battalion Scouts under 2nd Lieut. C.S.Lewis will advance at 9am. via SOUTH WEALD and NOAK'S HILL.

Advance Guard. 4."A" Company under Capt.G.Strongitharm will form the Advance Guard.

5.The Battalion will parade at 9.30a.m. on the INGRAVE ROAD at its junction with the LONDON ROAD, and advance via SOUTH WEALD and NOAK's HILL to HAVERING-ATTE-BOWER and will take up a defensive position from the bend in the road (inclusive) immediately W of the letter H in HAVERING (on the right) to the letter A in HAVERING PARK on the left.
A.B. & D.Companies forming the outpost line. C Company in reserve.

6.The Machine Gun Officer (2ndLt.A.W. Tratman) will report suitable gun positions

7. Reports to be sent to the head of the main body en route, afterwards to the Church, HAVERING-ATTE-BOWER.

(Signed) R.Lowther Lieut.
A/Adjutant 2/6th.Bn.Gloster Regt.,

Issued by Orderly at 6a.m.

Copy	No.1	Filed.
"	No.2	O.C."A"Coy.
"	No.3	O.C."B"Coy.
"	No.4	O.C."C"Coy.
"	No.5	O.C."D"Coy.
"	No.6	M.G.O.
"	No.7	Signalling Officer.
"	No.8	Scout Officer.

NOTE.

Men will not be deployed during this exercise. Officers will proceed to the outpost position (while the men are cooking dinners in their messtins), and will prepare rapid field skethhes and reports; these should be ready in about ¾ of an hour.
IT IS TO BE UNDERSTOOD THAT THE BATTALION IS OF THE FULL STRENGTH OF 850.

Appendix 1.

Subject:- Tactical Exercise on January 23th.1916

2/6th.Batt.The Gloucester Regiment.

REGIMENTAL EXERCISE JANUARY 13th. 1916.

(Reference ½" O.S. Sheet 30)

GENERAL IDEA.

An invading Force of all arms has advanced from SOUTHEND and on the night 12/13th.January has obtained possession of the Railway and occupied ROMFORD and BRENTWOOD.

''''''''''''''''''''''''''''''''''''

SPECIAL IDEA.

THE 2/6th.Bn. Gloster Regt., which has billeted for the night at BRENTWOOD under Command of Lieut.Colonel T.M.Carter is ordered to be at HAVERING-ATTE- BOWER at 12 noon and to take up a defensive position N.E. of that Town.

Subject :- Tactical Exercise. on Jan 14/16th. Appendix 2.

FROM

Headquarters.
183rd Infantry Brigade.

Brentwood. 10.1.16.

The Brigade will take part in a Tactical Exercise on Friday next the 14th.inst.,

Reference ½" O.S.Sheet 30.

General Idea. On the night 13/14 January 1916 the 61st. Division is billeted in the neighbourhood of BRENTWOOD. An invading force of all arms has landed at SOUTHEND and is moving on BILLERICAY with the apparent intention of cutting the LONDON main line railway.

SPECIAL IDEA. A Column composed of :-

2/1st. R.F.A. Brigade.
183rd.Infantry Brigade.
2/3rd.(South Midland) Field Ambulance.

under the Command of COL.SIR JOHN BARNSLEY V.D. is ordered to be at BILLERICAY at 11a.m. on the morning of January 14th.1916, to take up a defensive position to the S.E. of that town, and to delay the enemy until the Division has taken up a defensive position among the main line of railway. Enemy Scouts were seen at RAYLEIGH at 8.0a.m. on January 14th.1916.

(Sgd) M.Marriott Major.

Brigade Major 183rd Infantry Brigade.

Appendix 2

OPERATION ORDER No.37. | C opy. No.
BY Col. SIR JOHN BARNSLEY V.D. | Brentwood.
COMMANDING 183rd Infantry Brigade. | 11.1.1916.

Reference ½" O.S. Sheet 30.

1.On the night 13/14 January 1916 the 61st.Division is billeted in the neighbourhood of BRENTWOOD.An invading force of all arms has landed at SOUTHEND and is moving on BILLERICAY with the apparent intention of cutting the LONDON main line of Railway.

2/1st.R.F.A.Bde.
183rd.Infantry Bde.
2/3rd.(South Midland) Field Ambulance

2.A column composed as per margin under the command of Col.Sir John Barnsley V.D. will be at BILLERICAY at 11a.m. on the morning of January 14th.1916 and take up a defensive position to the S.E. of that Town,delaying the enemy until the Division has taken up a defensive position along the main line of railway.

3. The column will rendezvous at the road Junction on the SHENFIELD - BILLERICAY road, at 10.45a.m. east of point 166.

2/1st.R.F.A. Bde.

4. The 2/1st.R.F.A.Bde.will proceed via LAWNESS. The remainder via SHENFIELD and HUTTON.

183rd Infantry Bde.
2/3rd(South Midland)
Field Ambulance.

5. The starting point for the 183rd Infantry Brigade & the 2/3rd.(South Midland) Field Ambulance will be on the BRENTWOOD-INGATESTONE road,at the Junction of the INGRAVE ROAD.

2 Companies 2/4th.
Gloucester Regt.

6. The advance guard composed as per margin will be ¾ mile ahead of main body.

Headquarters
183rd Infantry Bde.
2/4th.Gloster Regt.
(less 2 Companies)
2/6th.Gloucester Regt.
2/7th.Worcester Regt.
2/8th.Worcester Regt.
183rd Infantry Bde.S.A.A. Reserve.
Brigaded Cookers and water Carts.
2/3rd (South Midland) Field Ambulance.

7. The head of the column,order as per margin,will pass the starting point at 9a.m.

8.The Brigade S.A.A.Reserve will be under the command of Major G.C.Gwynne 2/4th.Gloucester Regt.
9.The Cookers and Water Carts will be Brigaded under an Officer to be detailed by the Brigade Transport Officer.
10.Each Battalion will detail 2 cyclist to report to the Advanced Guard at starting point at 8.40a.m.
11.All messages to be sent to Headquarters at the head of the column.

(sd)M.Marriott Major. Bde.Major 183rd.Inf.Bde

Appendix 3.

OPERATION ORDERS BY

Lieut. Colonel T.M.Carter. Copy No.

Commanding 2/6th.Bn.Gloucester Regt.,

Ref: O.S. 1" Sheet 108

Brentwood.
19.1.1916.

2/6th.Bn.Gloster Regiment.	1. The force as per margin is ordered to hold the village of Pilgrims HATCH against a force advancing from the direction of ONGAR.
Scouts..	2. The Battalion Scouts under 2nd.Lt.C.S. Lewis will advance at 5.45pm. and reconnoitre PILGRIMS HATCH and all country within lines drawn between cross roads at PILGRIMS HATCH - cross roads W of WISHFIELD FARM - Point 283 - PILGRIMS HATCH.
Advance Guard.	3. C Company under Captain R.W.G.Cox will form the advance guard.
	4. The Battalion will parade on the INGRAVE ROAD at Junction BRENTWOOD - INGATESTONE ROAD with INGRAVE ROAD at 6.0pm.and proceed to PILGRIMS HATCH via BRENTWOOD - ONGAR ROAD.
	5. Reports will be sent to the head of the main body.

(Sgd) R.A.Young Captain.

Adjutant 2/6th.Bn.Gloster Regt.,

Issued by Orderly at 4.30p.m. 19.1.1916.

Copy No.1 Filed.
: 2 O.C. A Co.
3 O.C. B Co.
4 O.C. C Co.
5 O.C. D Co.
6 O.C. M.Gun Section.
7 O.C. Scouts.
8 O.C. Signallers.

""""""""""""""""""""""""""""""

Appendix 3.

G E N E R A L   I D E A .

Brentwood. 19.1.1916.

A Brigade advancing N.W. from the neighbourhood of HORNDON - on - the - HILL has reached BRENTWOOS on the afternoon of January 19th. and an attack is expected by troops in the neighbourhood of ONGAR.

S P E C I A L   I D E A .

The 2/6th.Bn. Gloucester Regiment is ordered to take up a position to hold PILGRIMS HATCH against attack from the North.

Appendix 4.

183rd Infantry Brigade.

General and Special Ideas for:-
Thursday January 27th. 1916.

- - - - - - - - - - - - - - - - - - - -

General Idea. An invading force of all arms, advancing on BRENTWOOD from the South has reached EAST HORNDON on the night of January 26th. and learning of the movement of troops in BRENTWOOD decides to take up an entrenched position on the South end of THORNDON PARK.

Special Idea. The following troops billeted in BRENTWOOD and INGATESTONE are ordered on the morning of January 27th. to attack the enemy in THORNDON PARK, and either destroy or capture him:-

2/1st. R.F.A.Bde.
183rd.Infantry Brigade.
2/3rd.(South Midland) Field Ambulance.

Object of exercise. Advance of infantry covered by Artillery fire, maintenance of direction and touch, fire discipline.

Place of assembly:-

S H E N F I E L D at 10a.m.

Appendix 4.

OPERATION ORDER No.38.

BY COL. SIR J.Barnsley V.D.

Commanding 183rd Infantry Brigade.

Reference 1" O.S. Sheet 108.

Copy No.

Brentwood.

27.1.1916.

---

1. An invading force of all arms reached EAST HORNDON on the night of Jan.26/17, and has taken up an entrenched position in the South end of THORNDON Pk.

2/1st.R.F.A.Bde.
183rd.Inf.Bde.
2/3rd.(S.M.)F.Amb.

2. A Force composed as per margin under the command of Col.Sir John Barnsley V.D.is order to attack the enemy and either destroy or capture him.

3. The place of assembly will be at SHENFIELD 10am. at the Junction of the SHENFIELF-BILLERICAY road with the main CHELMSFORD-LONDON road by the second N in INN

4. The route will be SHENFIELD-PRIEST LANE (the road cutting the D in BRENTWOOD)-SHENFIELD COMMON-INGRAVE GREEN.

5. The starting point for 183rd.Infantry Bde.& 2/3rd. (S.M.)F.Amb.will be on the LONDON -CHELMSFORD road at the cross roads West of B in BRENTWOOD.

2 Coys.
2/6th.Glouc.R.

6. The Advance Guard composed as per margin will be ½ mile ahead of main body.

Hdqrs.183rd.Inf/Bde
2/6th.Glos.Regt.
(less2 Coys.)
2/7th.Worcs.Regt.
2/8th.Worcs.Regt.
2/4th.Glouc.Regt.
183rd.Inf.Bde.S.A.A.Res.
2/3rd (S.M.) Fld.Amb.

7. The head of the main will pass the starting point at 9.45a.m. Order of march as per margin.

8. The Brigade S.A.A. Reserve will be under the Command of Major G.C.Gwynne 2/4th.Gloster Regt.

9. Each Battalion will detail 2 Cyclists to report to O.C. Advance Guard at starting point at 9.30am.

10. All messages to be sent to Headquarters at the Head of column.

(Sgd) M.Marriott Major.
Bde.Major 183rd.Infantry Brigade.

Copy No.1 to 2/1st.R.F.A. by post.
Copy No.2 to 2/4th.Glos.Re. by orderly.
3. to 2/6th.Glos.Re. " "
4. to 2/7th.Worc.Re. " "
5. to 2/8th.Worc.Re. " "
6. to 2/3rd.(SM)Fld.Amb.by orderly.

C O N F I D E N T I A L.

W A R.D I A R Y.

of

2/6th. Battalion Gloucestershire Regiment.

FROM 23rd. May 1916. TO 31st. May 1916.

(Volume 1.)

May '16
Feb '18

Instructions regarding War Diaries and Intelligence Summaries are contained in F. S. Regs., Part II. and the Staff Manual respectively. Title pages will be prepared in manuscript.

WAR DIARY 2/6 Glos. Regt.

~~or~~

~~INTELLIGENCE SUMMARY.~~

(*Erase heading not required.*)

Army Form C. 2118.

Page 1.

Place	Date	Hour	Summary of Events and Information	Remarks and references to Appendices
TIDWORTH	23.5.16		Entrained for FRANCE, Embarked SOUTHAMPTON for HAVRE, Personnel on the ST MARGUERITE & Transport on the BELLEROPHON were unable to reach HAVRE that night owing to there being submarines off HAVRE	APPENDIX A Ray.
The St MARGUERITE	24.5.16		Re-embarked SOUTHAMPTON 5.15 p.m, Sailed 6 p.m.	Ray.
HAVRE	25th	10 p.m	Disembarked HAVRE 8 a.m & marched to REST CAMP No 5.	Ray.
BUSNES.	26th		Entrained HAVRE 9.15 a.m	Ray.
-do-	27th	1 p.m.	Arrived BERGUETTE 9 a.m & marched to Billets at BUSNES.	Ray.
-do-	28th	11.30 a.m	Church Parades, The Corps Commander called a meeting of all officers of the 183 Bde 5.30 p.m	Ray.
-do-			at the HOTEL de VILLE ST VENANT.	Ray.
-do-	29th 31st	1 a.m	Army Commander (1st Army) inspected the Brigade at ST VENANT.	
-do-			At 11.25 p.m a test alarm was given	Ray.
-do-	30th	7 p.m.	Company & detail Training.	Ray.
Cin MAR MUSE	31st	8 p.m.	Marched from BUSNES to LA Cix MARMUSE.	Ray

Thos McCarter.

Lieut. Col. Commanding 2/6 Glos. Regt.

1577 Wt. W10791/1773 500,000 1/15 D. D. & L. A.D.S.S./Forms/C. 2118.

Instructions regarding War Diaries and Intelligence Summaries are contained in F. S. Regs., Part II. and the Staff Manual respectively. Title pages will be prepared in manuscript.

WAR DIARY ~~or~~ 2/6 Glos. Regt.

~~INTELLIGENCE SUMMARY.~~

(Erase heading not required.)

Army Form C. 2118.

APPENDIX. A

Place	Date	Hour	Summary of Events and Information	Remarks and references to Appendices

Train No.	Officers	Warrant Officers	Sergeants	Cpls	L/Cpls	Drummers	Ptes	Depart Tidworth	Arrive Southampton
X1443.	17	3	27	20	37	8	362	11.45 a.m.	1.25 p.m.
X1445.	17	3	24	17	40	8	362	12.50 p.m.	2.25 p.m.

HORSES.

	Riding	Draught	Pack	Mules.
1st Train	7	19.	4	[illegible]
2nd Train	5	18	3	6.

VEHICLES

	Cycles	4 wheeled	2 wheeled
1st Train	6	9	2.
2nd Train	3	8	2.

1577 Wt. W10791/1773 500,000 1/15 D. D. & L. A.D.S.S./Forms/C. 2118.

61

Vol II

Confidential

War Diary

of:

2/6 Bn. Gloucestershire Regt.

From 1 June 1916. To 30 June 1916.

Volume 2.

H. 2

Instructions regarding War Diaries and Intelligence Summaries are contained in F. S. Regs., Part II. and the Staff Manual respectively. Title pages will be prepared in manuscript.

WAR DIARY 2/6 Glos. Regt. Vol II

or

~~INTELLIGENCE SUMMARY.~~

(Erase heading not required.)

Army Form C. 2118.

Page 1

Place	Date	Hour	Summary of Events and Information	Remarks and references to Appendices
LA CIX MARMUSE	1.6.16	7 p.m.	Battalion in Divisional Reserve (35th Div) working parties, 4 officers + 36 N.C.O.s & men sent to Bombing School, Engineering School 4 officers + 20 N.C.O.s, 1 officer + 24 N.C.O.s + men on Lewis Gun Course, Sniping Course 1 officer, 1 N.C.O. + 9 men, remainder of B.N. on working parties	RAY
-do-	2.6.16	10 p.m.	Same as on the 1st. Two officers + 100 N.C.O.s + men sent to RICHEBOURG St VAAST	RAY
-do-	3.6.16	8.30 p.m.	Same as on the 2nd	
-do-	4.6.16	10 p.m.	Same as on the 3rd	RAY
-do-	5.6.16	7 p.m.	Same as on the 4th	RAY
-do-	6.6.16	7 p.m.	Same as on the 5th LIEUT. COL. T.M. CARTER proceeded to England + MAJOR R.E. BOULTON assumed Command of the B.N.	RAY
-do-	7.6.16	10 p.m.	Same as on the 6th	RAY
RICHEBOURG ST VAAST	8.6.16	11 p.m.	The Battalion moved to RICHEBOURG ST VAAST, two Companies (B + C) went into the line for instruction	Appendix 1 RAY.
-do-	9.6.16	12 p.m.	Received orders to move to PONT DU HEM on 10.6.16	RAY
PONT DU HEM.	10.6.16	7 p.m.	Arrived PONT DU HEM 12 noon + billeted the B.N. Received orders to take over MOTED GRANGE Section from 13th B.N. R.W.F.	RAY
WINCHESTER HOUSE	11.6.16	11 p.m.	Took over trenches from 13th R.W.F. relief commenced 8.30 p.m. + was complete 10.50 p.m.	RAY
			Asked gunners for a test shot at 2.10 a.m., shot fired 2.13 p.m. on night lines.	RAY

1577 Wt. W10791/1773 500,000 1/15 D. D. & L. A.D.S.S./Forms/C. 2118.

Instructions regarding War Diaries and Intelligence Summaries are contained in F. S. Regs., Part II. and the Staff Manual respectively. Title pages will be prepared in manuscript.

WAR DIARY 2/6 Glos. Regt.

~~or~~

~~INTELLIGENCE SUMMARY.~~

(Erase heading not required.)

Army Form C. 2118.

Page 2.

Place	Date	Hour	Summary of Events and Information	Remarks and references to Appendices
WINCHESTER HOUSE.	12.6.16.	11 p.m.	Very quiet, wind S.S.W. Huns were seen over parapet wearing round blue caps with thin red band round centre.	RAY.
	13.6.16	12.50 am	Hun very quiet. Received orders re change of Brigade front.	Appendix 2
			Following wire received from Brigade. "XI Corps wires begins aaa MAJOR L.A.C. HAMILTON 1st BATTALION SCOTTISH RIFLES to command 2/6 GLOS REGT vice LIEUT. COL. T.M. CARTER aaa	
			Working parties for R.E.	Appendix 3. RAY.
	14.6.16.	11.30 pm	Man seen working in civilian clothes in rear of crater on new sap at M.30.c.5.0.	
			3 Enemy's 4.2's fell at 2.30 p.m in M.24 between ERITH KEEP & GLOUCESTER HOUSE	
			~~..~~ Wind N.W. mod dropping at night.	RAY.
			One man killed, + one wounded.	RAY.
	15.6.16	11 p.m.	Enemy working party carrying material along tramway about M30.B.0.5 - MGO informed also heavy timber carrying at M.30.B.0.5. Three snipers posts M.30.a.4½ and M.30.A.5.3. and with M.G. Emplacement at M.24.d.6.3½, ~~...~~ Snipers claim two victims (certain)	RAY

1577 Wt. W10791/1773 500,000 1/15 D. D. & L. A.D.S.S./Forms/C. 2118.

Page 3

WAR DIARY 2/6 Glos. Regt. Army Form C. 2118.

~~or~~

~~INTELLIGENCE SUMMARY.~~

(Erase heading not required.)

Instructions regarding War Diaries and Intelligence Summaries are contained in F. S. Regs., Part II. and the Staff Manual respectively. Title pages will be prepared in manuscript.

Place	Date	Hour	Summary of Events and Information	Remarks and references to Appendices
Trenches.				
	15.6.16	11 p.m.	Sent out two Patrols. Our Artillery damaged Enemy's parapet & Crater at M.30.a.4.4. with Shrapnell & 4.2's from noon till 1.30 p.m	
			Continued work on New Trench at M.29.b.10.2.	
			Signals Seen	Appendix 3
			Wind N.N.E. Light	
	16.6.16	11.30 p.m.	Snipers report Enemy transport line on rd. N.25 c 5.0. moving S. at 9.15 p.m.	
			Large Enemy working party M.30 B 8 4. on new work previously noted. R.F.A. informed	
			Snipers obtained one victim (certain)	
			Signals 9.30 p.m String of white lights twice repeated in rapid succession.	
			Reconnoitring Patrols under 2nd Lt T. T. Pryce reports "going Easy" opposite M.24 c.8 1 & 6 P in Sap M30.B1.8	
			Working party completed wire outside our parapet with covering party.	
			No 1413 Sgt Jones (Sniper) was shot about 12.30 p.m.	
			Wind N.E.	[illegible]

Instructions regarding War Diaries and Intelligence Summaries are contained in F. S. Regs., Part II. and the Staff Manual respectively. Title pages will be prepared in manuscript.

WAR DIARY ~~or~~ 2/6 Glos. Regt.

~~INTELLIGENCE SUMMARY.~~

(*Erase heading not required.*)

Army Form C. 2118.

Page 4.

Place	Date	Hour	Summary of Events and Information	Remarks and references to Appendices
MOTED GRANGE SECTION.	17.6.16	11.45pm.	Casualties nil. Wind E by N 18 miles per hr. Intelligence	RAY. Appendix 4.
-do-	18.6.16	10pm	Casualties Killed No 4957 Pte JAMES, No 4946 Pte HANCOCK + No 3706 Cpl MOUNTFORD. Seven	
-do-			wounded. Wind N.N.E light. Intelligence attached.	Appendix 5 RAY.
-do-	19.6.16	11p.m	Wind N.E. changing E. Tactical Progress.	Appendix 6 RAY.
-do-	20.6.16	11p.m.	Operations orders re move to LA GORGUE	Appendix 7 RAY.
LA GORGUE.	21.6.16	12pm	Marched to Billets at LA GORGUE.	RAY
-do-	22.6.16	10p.m.	Inspections, Baths.	RAY
-do-	23.6.16	8pm	Training.	RAY
-do-	24.6.16	11p.m	Training	RAY
-do-	25.6.16	9pm	Church Parades.	RAY
-do-	27.6.16	10pm	Training	RAY
-do-	28.6.16	9.p.m	F.G.C.M. on No 4809 Pte H S DOLMAN Sec 6(1b) AA. F.G.C.M. on No 5014 Pte F.W. THOMAS charge Sec(6.1c) AA.	RAY.
HOBERMETZ	29.6.16		Training at LA GORGUE	PHB
do	30.6.16		do	PHB

In The Field. 14.8.16.

F. A. [illegible] Major.
2/6. Gloucestershire Regt.

T2134. Wt. W708—776. 500000. 4/15. Sir J. C. & S.

S E C R E T .

2/6th Battalion Gloster Regiment. APPENDIX I.

OPERATION ORDERS NO.1 BY MAJOR R.E.BOULTON COMMANDING.

7.6.1916.

1. The Battalion will relieve the 2/7th Battalion Worcester Regiment in the FERME DU BOIS Section to-morrow, June 8th 1916.

2. All Specialists will do duty in the ranks, except Headquarters Signallers, who will be attached to Battalion Headquarters.

3. "A" Company will be attached to 17th Lan. Fus.
"B" Company will be attached to 23rd Manchesters.
"C" Company will be attached to 18th Lan. Fus.
"D" Company will be attached to 17th Lan. Fus.

"A" Company and Headquarters parade Battalion Headquarters 10.30 a.m. Guides will meet them at S. 2 c.o.8, at 2 p.m.

"B" Company parade 5.30 p.m. and will be met by Guides at X. 17. c.6.7. at 8.30 p.m.

"C" Company parade 5.30 p.m., and will be met by Guides at S. 2. c. o.8, at 8.30 p.m.

"D" Company parade 11 a.m., and will be met by Guides at X. 5. a. 3.0., at 2 p.m.

Companies will march off with a distance of 200 yards between platoons, subject to changes by order of Control Posts.

(Signed) R.A.YOUNG Captain.

Adjutant 2/6th Battalion Gloster Regiment.

APPENDIX 2.

SECRET.

PRELIMINARY ORDER.

Arrangements will be made to carry out the following at an early date, probably 15th June.

1. 183rd Infantry Brigade will take over part of the NEUVE CHAPELLE section from the 35th DIVISION as far as OXFORD STREET S.5c.4.6. and will hold the line with three Battalions, a and one in Reserve.

2. 7th WORCESTERS will take over the new Section from the Battalion of the 105th BRIGADE.

3. 4th GLOUCESTERS will move from Billets in Riez to reserve Billets at RUE du FRUITS M.26.d.5.5. with Battalion Headquarters at M.26.d.8.7.

4. Brigade Headquarters will move to LES HUIT MAISON M.29.d.88.

5. The Officer Commanding 7th Worcesters will make all arrangements with the Battalion 105th Brigade to take over and arrangements as to guides etc.

6. Orders for Machine Gun Company and Trench Mortar Batteries will be detailed later.

13.6.1916.

(Sd.) R.R. Mowatt Major.
Brigade Major, 183rd Infantry Brigade.

Appendix 3

W O R K I N G   P A R T I E S .

The following Working Parties will be found daily until further Orders.

"B" COMPANY. NO. 15.
Working Party - 40 Other Ranks.

BIRD CAGE M.30.a.2.5. 9p.m. until 1a.m. - report to Lieut. Gibbs, R.E. This party will not take tools, rations or equipment, but will carry 50 rounds of Ammunition per man in pockets.

Covering party required. Work on New Advanced Trench.

"A" COMPANY. NO. 16.
Working Party - 10 Other Ranks.

WINCHESTER COMMUNICATION TRENCH - Trench End - M.30.a.4.9. - 9.30p.m. until 1a.m. under Lieut. Cornelius. R.E. for work on Trench Mortar Emplacements. This Party will not take tools or rations.

"A" COMPANY NO. 1.
Working Party - 12 Other Ranks

WINCHESTER COMMUNICATION TRENCH - Trench End - 9.15a.m. until 4p.m. Work on Steel Dugouts under Lieut. Hosegood. Haversack Rations will be carried.

"C" COMPANY NO. 2.
Working Party - 20 Other Ranks

Trench End - WINCHESTER COMMUNICATION TRENCH - 9.15a.m. until 4pm.m. Work on Stores Depot under Lieut. Cornelius. R.E. Haversack Rations will be carried.

"D" COMPANY NO. 4.
Working Party - 1 Officer

30 Other Ranks - GRANTS POST - 9.15a.m. until 4pm.m Work on Reserve Line under Lieut. Hosegood. R.E. Haversack Rations will be carried.

(Signed) R.A. YOUNG. Captain.

Adjutant. 2/6th. Battalion Gloster Regiment.

APPENDIX 3.

Extract from Tactical Progress Report from 8 am 15.6.16 to 8 am 16.6.16.

SIGNALS.

1.15 a.m. rocket showing red and white light. The following lights were seen in the rear of the German line:-

9.35 p.m. 3 green followed by 2 red.
10.0 p.m. red, red, pause, red.
10.10 p.m. red, pause, green.
10.15 p.m. 8 red in succession.

R.C. Young Capt
Adjt

APPENDIX 4.

Tactical Progress Report 8 am 17/616 to 8 am 18/616.

Part 1 - Intelligence.

Enemy Working Parties:
On parapet 4 a.m. M.30a.9.5.
At SHRINE N.25 a.4.6. from 12 noon to 4 p.m. - 6 men also seen leaving SHRINE at 8 p.m.

Dress: 2 round soft caps (no peak) dark grey - light grey band - small round white metal badge.

Aeroplanes: 11.30 a.m. 17/6/16 - fight over enemy lines - no decisive result.

Observation balloon up from 12 noon to 8 p.m.

Officers patrol report enemy patrol 15 (about) strong, 10.45 p.m. M.30.b.½.7 - another 6 at M.24.d.1.0.
Signals - 11.10 p.m. red lights about M.30 (centre) 2.30 a.m. One green.
Gas - At 12.45 a.m. the alarm was taken up from the left. No taste of gas however was reported in the area.

Part 11 - Operations.

Officers Patrol under Capt. D.B.Coates and 2/Lt.T.T.Pryce went out for the purpose of reconnoitreing the enemy's wire ~~(report attached)~~ together with standing patrol of 3 men under Lieut. Fison - the patrol was unable to get near the wire owing to meeting two large parties of the enemy. ~~Patrol reports attached.~~

New trench N. & S. of M.30.a.0.1. with a covering party of 1 Officer and 10 men. Additions repairs and wiring in ERITH, TILLELOY and DREADNOUGHT Posts. Support line improved and damage repaired in Traffic Trench.

R.W. Young Capt
Adjt.

Appendix 5.

Tactical Progress Report from 8 a.m. 18/6/16 - 8 a.m. 19/6/16.

Part 1 - Intelligence.

Enemy's wire has been strengthened round about M.30.a.5.5.
2 enemy observation balloons up from noon to 2 p.m.
At 9 p.m. enemy party 30 (counted) seen again walking from SHRINE N.25.a.4.6. and 5 men wearing white badges and carrying no arms or equipment - dispersed by our machine guns at 9.15 - Casualties uncertain owing to fading light.
Cockade was seen White Green White (Saxon) and a light grey uniform in front line - soft round cap blue-grey.
In spite of very careful observation the past 7 days little evidence of life appears in the front line by day - only at rare intervals heads have been seen. It appears therefore to be very thinly held by day.
Signals: Red and white lights sent up at 1.30 after commencement of artillery activity.

Part 2 - Operations.

Artillery activity on both sides from 1.15 to 2.30 a.m.
Officers patrol under 2/Lieut. T.T.Pryce (attached) report enemy wire about M.24.d.42. for 130 yards-to be concertinas 7 ft. high in places - generally not deep - 2 ft.

Part 3 - Work.

Repairing and wiring parapets - Reserve trenches & Keeps - 15 yards new wire sector M.30.2.
T.Ms. and M.G.Cos. not yet to hand.

R.E. Evans Capt
& Adj.

APPENDIX 6.

Tactical Progress Report from 8 a.m. 19.6.16 to 8 a.m. 20.6.16.

Part 1 - Intelligence.

Snipers Report M.G. at M.24.c.9½.3½.
Enemy parapet appears to have been damaged by our artillery during the day about M.30.c.55.57.
Replacement of old Grenades by new well oiled stuff nearly complete, those which have been in the LINE for sometime are thought tobe probably partially unserviceable.

Part 2 - Operations.

3 Patrols went out, 2 for the purpose of examining our wire, and reporting defects, third to ascertain whether damage done, the previous night, to enemy's wire had been repaired. The Patrol was unable to complete the reconnaisance owing to lack of time, and meeting enemy Patrol.

R W Young Capt
Adj

Battalion Routine Orders No. II (Continued).

7. WOUNDED IN ACTION (Continued).

2532 Pte. H.Evans "A" Company (4th Essex Regt. attd.) 13.6.16.
1690 " A.Clark "A" Company (6th Devon Regt. attd.) 13.6.16.
4049 " W.J.Stone "B" Company 13.6.16.

8. KILLED IN ACTION.
The following were killed in action on dates shewn against their names, and are struck off the strength from thoese dates:-
4755 Pte. T.H.Davey "A" Company 13.6.16.
1912 Serjt. E.J.Jones "D" Company 13.6.16.

9. INJURED AT DUTY.
No. 1393 Cpl. F. Richards "B" Company was injured on 13.6.16 in the execution of his duties.

10. TUNNELLING COMPANY - DETACHMENT.
The following have been detailed to join the Tunnelling Company (36th Division), and are detached from this Unit from 11.6.1916:-

"A" Company.

2163 Drmr. W.Alder
5919 Pte. T.Myers.
2929 " G.A.Ashmead (1st Hereford Reg . attd.)
3234 " E.Jacques.
4720 " W.H.Carpenter.
2811 " G.Williams (1st Hereford Regt. attd.)
3247 " G.W.Williams do. do.
4016 " A.Riddick.
2176 " F.Bowden (D.C.L.I. attd.)
2977 L/cpl. A.J.Crane (4th Essex Regt. attd.)
2349 Pte. J.Webb (1st Hereford Regt. attd.)
4711 " G.F.Staddon.

"B" Company.

4895 Pte. E.W.Allen.
4386 " W.G.Bodman.
2083 " A.V.Berry (6th Devon Regt. attd.)
2009 " W.Baker do. do.
1985 " A.Braund do. do.
3384 " J.Luxton.
4868 " R.Alford.
5015 " G.S.Derrick.
4060 " T.McKay.
4967 " L.E.Jones.
4749 " W.Mathews.
4903 " S.Elliott.

"C" Company.

2462 L/cpl. A.E.Pritchard.
3742 Pte. G.H.Wright.
3713 " S.J.Loriot (4th Essex Regt. attd.)
1618 " G.P.Mock (6th Devon Regt. attd.)
4715 " G.J.W.Tooze.
3146 " W.J.Nash (4th Essex Regt. attd.)
4948 L/cpl. E.Hutton.
4968 Pte. C.W.Vesey.
4786 " J.A.Holmes.
2492 " F.S.Hubbard (4th Essex Regt. attd.)
2820 " L.Hill.
3916 " H.C.Baker.

(Sd) R.A.YOUNG. Captain.

Adjutant, 2/6th Bn. Gloster Regt.

APPENDIX 7.

SECRET. 1. Copy No. 2.

2/6th Battalion Gloster Regiment.

OPERATION ORDER NO. 1. 20.6.16.

1. The 182nd Brigade will relieve the 183rd Brigade on the 21st June, and night of 21/22nd June 1916.

2. Companies of the 2/7th Warwickshire Regiment will take over positions occupied by Companies of this Unit.

3. The relief will commence at 9 p.m.

4. All movement of troops along, or east of the BELLE CROIX - LA BASSEE ROAD, will be by platoons at 50 yards distance. Wagons and carts will move by threes at the same distance.

5. Details mentioned in 61st Div. Trench Standing Orders No. 19 B., together with Lewis Gun Teams, and Battalion Signallers, will report at Battalion Headquarters at 3 p.m.

6. Great care will be taken to obtain receipts for all stores etc. handed over. All ammunition (S.A.A. & Very), and grenades, are to be counted by boxes - a broken box should be so stated on the receipt. Receipts will be forwarded in duplicate to Battalion Headquarters by 9 a.m. 22.6.1916.

7. Front Line Companies, i.e. "B", "D" and "C", will send guides, one per platoon, to report at Battalion Trench Headquarters at 8.15 p.m.
   Attached Company 8th Worcester Regiment will send one guide for each platoon in Reserve Line, and one guide for each Post to report at same time and place.

8. Order in which Companies will be relieved is Reserve Company, (8th Worcesters), "D", "B", "C" Companies.

9. Incoming platoons will move into front trenches by WINCHESTER TRENCH, into Reserve by ERITH TRENCH, except for TILLELOY and WINCHESTER POSTS.
   Outgoing platoons will leave trenches, "D" "B" and "C" Companies by WINCHESTER STREET: Reserve Company (except TILLELOY and WINCHESTER POSTS), by ERITH TRENCH.
   Each platoon or post of Reserve Company, will move out as soon as relieved. "D" and "B" Companies will not leave their trenches until the Company ~~until the Company~~ relieving "C" Company has cleared WINCHESTER STREET. "D" Company will be responsible for ascertaining when "C" Company relief has cleared WINCHESTER STREET, and will then move out followed by "B" Company: 50 yards distance between platoons. "C" Company will move out in same manner after relief.

10. Each Company Commander before leaving his Trench Headquarters, will telephone the word "PARIS" as signifying that relief is complete.

11. Officers Trench Kits and other Company baggage, will be taken to trench railhead and trollies moved off at 10 p.m. to Epinette where transport will be waiting. Officer Commanding Reserve Company to make his own arrangements.
    Baggage parties of Companies to form up, after loading Company baggage, at EPINETTE, march to billets under Serjt. H.Tucker No. 2471.

12. Route: LA FLINQUE Cross Roads - PONT DU HEM - LA GORGUE.

12 (Continued). Companies will form up at road junction north of PONT DU HEM, where the LAVENTIE ROAD joins the LABASSEE - ESTAIRES ROAD, and will march independently ~~xxx~~ to billets.

13. Battalion Headquarters will close at WINCHESTER HOUSE on completion of relief, and will re-open at LA GORGUE.

HOUR OF ISSUE - 2 p.m.

R.A. Evans

Captain & Adjutant
2/5th Bn. Gloster Regiment.

Copy No. 1 File.
No. 2 War Diary.
No. 3 "B" Company.
No. 4 "C" "
No. 5 "D" "
No. 6 Supports (2/8th Bn. Worcester Regt.)

61

Vol III

Confidential.

War Diary

of 2/6 Bn. Gloucestershire Regt.

From 1st July. 1916 To 31st July. 1916.

Volume 3.

2/6 Bn. GLOUCESTERSHIRE Regt.

1

Army Form C. 2118.

WAR DIARY
or
~~INTELLIGENCE SUMMARY.~~
(Erase heading not required.)

Instructions regarding War Diaries and Intelligence Summaries are contained in F. S. Regs., Part II. and the Staff Manual respectively. Title pages will be prepared in manuscript.

Place	Date	Hour	Summary of Events and Information	Remarks and references to Appendices
	1916			
LAGORGUE	July 1	10 p.m.	Training. C.O. & O.C. Coys. to LAVENTIE re move to reserve billets	PHB
do	2	8 p.m.	Church Parade. Arrangements re move.	PHB
LAVENTIE	3	11 p.m.	Move to LAVENTIE	APP. 1. PHB
do	4	–	Working Parties. Coy. raid of Bn. in front line.	PHB
do	5		Working Parties.	PHB
do	6		do ~~8 Officers from 11th Devon Regt.~~	PHB
do	7		do	PHB
do	8		do 8 Officers from 11th Devon Regt.	PHB
do	9		Relief of 2/4th GLOSTERS in FAUQUISSART SECTION	APP. 2 PHB
TRENCHES Nr FAUQUISSART	10		TRENCHES. Preparations for raid	PHB
"	11		do	PHB
"	12		do	PHB
"	13 14		do All preparation for GAS ATTACK. Wind failed & attack cancelled.	PHB PHB
"	15		Bn. relieved by 2/4 GLOSTERS & 2/4 R. BERKS. Billets at LAVENTIE	PHB
"	16		Move into trenches to take over part of line from 2/4 GLOSTERS	PHB
"	17		Awaiting orders to attack – orders cancelled pending further preparation.	PHB

T2134. Wt. W708—776. 500000. 4/15. Sir J. C. & S.

2

Army Form C. 2118.

Instructions regarding War Diaries and Intelligence Summaries are contained in F. S. Regs., Part II. and the Staff Manual respectively. Title pages will be prepared in manuscript.

WAR DIARY
or
~~INTELLIGENCE SUMMARY.~~
(Erase heading not required.)

Place	Date	Hour	Summary of Events and Information	Remarks and references to Appendices
TRENCHES Nr LAVENTIE	July 18		Trenches. Attack still postponed. Carrying parties &c.	G.H.B.
"	" 19		Bombardment of E. Trenches 11 a.m. Return bombardment - about 50 casualties. First wave of two platoons left trenches at 5.40 p.m. Barrage lifted 7 &c. Two more waves & part of 4th went out. Men practically blown back as they went over parapet by machine gun & shrapnel. Withdrawn about 7 o'clock. Artillery turned on E. front line again. 8 &c orders received to attack again at 9 p.m. 8.20 p.m. orders received cancelling attack. 9 p.m. orders received to prepare for relief by 2/7 WORCESTERS. Relief complete 2 a.m. Total casualties 13 officers 165 O.R. LIEUT-COL HAMILTON was wounded at 6 pm. MAJOR BARTLEET assumed command.	APP. 3 G.H.B.
LEVANTIE	20		Rested & reformed companies.	G.H.B.
	21		Reforming & equipping Companies. Short route march } Carrying parties.	G.H.B.
	22		Inspection by G.O.C. Carrying parties	G.H.B.
	23		Rest. Carrying parties & R.E. working parties.	G.H.B.
	24		Training. Carrying parties.	G.H.B.

T2134. Wt. W708—776. 500000. 4/15. Sir J. C. & S.

Instructions regarding War Diaries and Intelligence Summaries are contained in F. S. Regs., Part II. and the Staff Manual respectively. Title pages will be prepared in manuscript.

3

Army Form C. 2118.

WAR DIARY
or
~~INTELLIGENCE SUMMARY.~~
(Erase heading not required.)

Place	Date	Hour	Summary of Events and Information	Remarks and references to Appendices
LEVANTIE	July 24		Took over unoccupied posts at ROAD BEND, WANGERIE & MASSELOT	APP 4. PHB
	25		Working parties	PHB
	26		do	PHB
	27		Three Posts as above taken over by 2/7 WORCESTERS. HOUGOMONT, DEAD END, PICANTIN & LEVANTIE E. taken over from 2/7 WORCESTERS. Dispositions of garrison of new post & ordered company for fulfilling picquet shewn on APP. 5	APP. 5 PHB
	28		Working parties	PHB
	29		do	PHB
	30		do	PHB
	31		do Orders received to relieve 2/4 GLOSTERS on Aug 1. 1916. CO. Adj & O.C. Coys visited their line to make necessary arrangements	PHB

A D Bartlett Major
Comdg
2/6 Bn. Gloucestershire Regt
1/8/16

T2134. Wt. W708—776. 500000. 4/15. Sir J. C. & S.

APPENDIX 1.

2/6th. Battalion Gloster Regiment.

ORDERS FOR MOVE INTO FORWARD BILLETS TO RELIEVE 2/4th. BATTALION BERKS. REGIMENT AT LA VENTIE.

July 3. 1916

1. The Battalion will move in the following order:-

(a) Portion of Battalion Headquarters under 2nd. Lieut. A.W.Tratman.	(Signallers except (2 Operators. (H.Q.Orderlies. (1 Despatch Rider.

(b) "D" Company.
(c) "C" Company.
(d) "B" Company.
(e) "A" Company.

(f) Lewis Gun Section with limbers.

(g) Police and Pioneers.

2. The Starting Piont is road junction near "A" Company Officers' Mess L.34.b.8.2: to be passed

(a) at 7.30a.m.
(b) " 7.37a.m.
(c) " 7.44a.m.
(d) " 7.51a.m.
(e) " 7.58a.m.
(f) " 8.5 a.m.
(g) " 8.12a.m.

Before moving East of the BELLE CROIX - LA BASSEE road G.32.a.2.1. Companies will break into Platoons moving with 100 yards distance between each.

3. Dress will be full Marching Order, steel helmets strapped on the pack.

4. Officers' baggage will be stacked in front of the Battalion Headquarter Officers' Mess by 7a.m. All Companies to detail 1 Officer's Servant each to remain in charge

Exception - "D" Company baggage will be collected from "D" Company Mess.

All Company Stores will be stacked, "A","B" and "C" by Bandstand, "D" at Company Headquarters ready for loading by 6a.m.

5. Companies will be roused at 5a.m.
Men's breakfast will be at 6.15a.m.
Field Kitchens will follow their own Companies.

6. Officers Commanding Companies and Special Sections are responsible that their billets are left clear of all refuse tins etc.

Each Company will detaila party of 1 N.C.O. and 4 men to report to Corporal Smale in the space behind "A" and "B" Company Billets at 5.30a.m.

7. No men other than authorized men of Transport are to ride on wagons, and all parties, however, small are to march as formed bodies.

8. All Company Quarter Master Serjeants. also 1 Other N.C.O. per Company will parade at the Bandstand at 6.30a.m., also 1 Despatch Rider to be detailed by the Officer i/c Signals, and 1 Policeman to be detailed by the R.S.M.

This party will form the Advanced Billeting Party and will move off under the Senior N.C.O. at 6.40a.m., to meet Captain XXXXXX Coates at LA VENTIE Level Crossing at 8a.m.

1 Copy

(Signed) P.H.Beck. Captain.
A/Adjutant. 2/6th. Battalion Gloster Regiment.

APPENDIX 2

2/6th Battalion The Gloucestershire Regiment.

MOVE TO TRENCHES. 8.7.16.

Movement will be by Sections at 10 minutes intervals during the day. All Sections are to be 10 minutes behind the preceding Section from the start.

"B" Company moves off :- 1st Platoon at 4.30 a.m.
2nd " " 5.10 a.m.
3rd " " 5.50 a.m.
4th " " 6.30 a.m.
2 Lewis Guns " 7.10 a.m.

1 Guide per Platoon and 1 Lewis Gun Guide from 2/4th Glos. Regt. will be at bend in road M.5.b.4.9 at 4.45 a.m.

Company to be relieved is right (D) Company of 2/4th Glos. Regt.

"A" Company moves off th occupy temporarily Posts now held by "C" Company i.e. MASSELOT: WANGERIE: ROAD BEND: via FORT ESQUIN :- 1st Platoon at 5.30 a.m.
2nd " " 6.10 a.m.
3rd " " 6.50 a.m.
4th " " 7.30 a.m.
1 Lewis Gun " 8.10 a.m.

"C" Company will have 1 Guide from each Platoon on the lookout for "A" Company at X Roads near WANGERIE.

"C" Company, after handing over Posts to "A" Company moves off :-
1st Platoon to reach entrance to GT. NORTH RD. at 7.30 a.m.
2nd " " " " 8.10 a.m.
3rd " " " " 8.50 a.m.
(4th " " " " 9.30 a.m.
((From LAVENTIE EAST)
2 Lewis Guns to reach entrance to GT. NORTH ROAD at 10.10 a.m.

Company to be relieved is "B"(right centre) Company 2/4th Glos. Regt. 1 Guide per Platoon will be at entrance to GT. NORTH RD. at 7.15 a.m., also 1 Lewis Gun Guide. Entrance to this trench is on RUE BACQUEROT.

"D" Company, after reliefe by "D" Company 2/4th Gloster Regt., moves forward :-
PICANTIN Platoon and 1 Lewis Gun 11 a.m.
DEAD END " 11.40 a.m.
HOUGOMONT " 12.20 p.m.
LAVENTIE E. " 12.45 p.m.

Company to be relieved is "C" (left centre) Company 2/4th Gloster Regt. Route is down PICANTIN Road. 1 Guide per Platoon and 1 Lewis Gun Guide will be on road near PICANTIN Post at 11 a.m.

O.C. "D" Company (Capt. Rudman) will arrange to send 1 Guide per Platoon and 1 Lewis Gun Guide forward with "B" Company (6th Gloseters) to Headquarters in front line of "D" (Right) Company (4th Glosters). These Guides will bring the Platoons of "D" Company 4th Glosters out to the various Posts.

An After Order will follow.

PH Beck
Capt.
A/Adjutant, 6th Glosters.

APPENDIX 3

SECRET. Copy No. 2.

183rd Brigade Order No. 23.

1. The 2/7th Worcesters will relieve the 2/4th Glosters and 2/6th Glosters in the trenches to-night.
The Headquarters of the 2/7th Worcesters will be at the present Battle Headquarters.

2. The O.C. 2/7th Worcesters will proceed to the Headquarters of the 2/4th and 2/6th Glosters, and make any necessary arrangements for the relief direct.

3. The 2/4th and 2/6th Glosters will endeavour to withdraw wounded from NO MAN'S LAND and the 2/4th Glosters any of their men from the enemy lines about X 16. For this purpose the centre group R.A. will continue a barrage on the enemy trenches at this point, and maintain fire on the front trench elsewhere. The 2/4th Glosters will arrange to send a patrol as soon as it is dark with the object of discovering if any of their men are in the enemy lines about X 16. Should it be previously ascertained that there are no men here, a report will at once be made to Brigade Headquarters.

4. The 183rd Trench Mortar Battery will withdraw 50% of their personnel into billets.

5. The 183rd Machine Gun Company will arrange to relieve the personnel which was in the trenches during the bombardment from their reserve. The normal of Guns will be kept in the front trenches, and any necessary arrangements made for indirect fire on the enemy's front opposite the 183rd Brigade.

6. R.E. Detachment will rejoin their Company.

7. "D" Company D.C.L.I. (Pioneers) will rejoin its Battalion.

8. Billetting parties to report to Staff Captain.

Issued at 9 p.m.

19/7/16

(Sd) M.M. Parry Jones Capt.
B.M. 183rd Brigade.

2/6th Battalion Gloucester Regiment. 8.7.1916.

1 Officer and 1 N.C.O. per Company will be sent into front line for taking-over purposes, to arrive there, from "C" Company at 7.30 a.m. from other Companies not later than 9 a.m.

Battalion Headquarter Signallers, less 2 Operators and 1 Despatch Rider, move off at 10.30 a.m. for new Batt. Headquarters.

Battalion Bombers and Snipers move off at 10 a.m. under Officers in charge.

The Lewis Gun Officer is to move with Lewis Guns moving with "B" Company at 7.10 a.m.

All Officers taking over Stores will keep a copy of what they take over, and will send a copy to Major Langford at Battalion Headquarters as soon as possible, and not later than 8 p.m. in any case.

Captain Rudman, Commanding "D" Company, is responsible for collecting the Platoon of "C" Company attached to him and causing it to reach entrance of GREAT NORTH ROAD Trench, first Section at 9.30 a.m.

Headquarter Details not mentioned will move at 2.30 p.m. for new Battalion Headquarters.

(Signed) F.A.C. HAMILTON. Lieut. Colonel.
Cmdg. 2/6th Battalion Gloucester Regiment.

APPENDIX 4

O.C. "C" Company.

OCCUPATION OF POSTS. 24. 7. 1916.

1. Your Company will Garrison the following posts to -day

ROAD BEND	-	1 Platoon.
WANGERIE	-	2 Platoon.
MASSELOT	-	1 Platoon.

2. In addition ~~to~~ one Lewis Gun will be detailed to ROAD BEND and one to WANGERIE.

3. Relief will proceed in parties of 7 at 10 minutes intervals via Ft. d'ESQUIN and RUE du BACQUEROT, the first party leaving your Headquarters at (6) p.m.

4. Lewis Gun Sections will follow your last party and have received their orders.

5. Report to be sent to Battn. Headquarters when occupation is completed, by using the word "DANDY".

6. Report to be sent to Battn. Headquarters by 9 a.m. 25.7.16 on the state of Posts, and as to whether the full complement of stores are there according to inventory boards.

7. 50% of the Garrison is available for work in or behind the Reserve Line, and details of working parties will be sent you.

8. Rations and Water Cart will be at WANGERIE daily at 6 a.m.

9. Casualty Return by 12 noon daily.
Return of work done daily by 9 a.m.
Return of Materials etc. required by 9 a.m.

A.D. Bartlett
Major.
Cmdg. 2/6th Bn. Glos. Regt.

APPENDIX 5

SECRET.

Extract from 183 Inf. Bde. B.M.563 27.7.1916:

<u>Disposition of Garrison in Post 27.7.16.</u>

HOUGOMONT) DEAD END) PICANTIN)	By 1 Coy from left Battn in Reserve (not less than 100 men).

LAVENTIE EAST - 4 Men.

These garrisons except those at ESQUIN & LAVENTIE EAST are at the disposal of Battn. Commander in sub-section concerned, and should be moved up into Reserve line from Stand-to to Stand-down, so as to be available for any counter-attacks.

Battns. in Reserve will, in addition, have 1 Company as Inlying Picquet, ready to go up and garrison the Posts at the shortest notice.

The Right Battn. in reserve will send 1 Platoon to ROAD BEND. 1 Platoon to WANGERIE. 2 Platoons to MASSELOT.

The left Battn. in reserve will send:

1 Platoon to HOUGOMONT.
2 Platoons to DEAD END.
1 Platoon to PICANTIN.

P.H. Beck
Capt
a/Adj.
2/6 Glosters

Vol 4

Confidential

War Diary

Of 2/6 Bn. GLOUCESTERSHIRE REGT.

From 1 Aug. 1916 To 31 Aug. 1916

Volume 2.

Page 1

Army Form C. 2118.

Instructions regarding War Diaries and Intelligence Summaries are contained in F. S. Regs., Part II. and the Staff Manual respectively. Title pages will be prepared in manuscript.

WAR DIARY
or
~~INTELLIGENCE SUMMARY.~~
2/6 Bn. GLOUCESTERSHIRE REGT.
(Erase heading not required.)

Place	Date	Hour	Summary of Events and Information	Remarks and references to Appendices
	1916			
LEVANTIE	Aug 1		Relief of 2/4 GLOSTERS complete 10.15 am.	APP I PHB
Nr. LAVENTIE Trenches	2		Trenches. v. quiet.	PHB
do	3		do	PHB
do	4		do orders received re relief.	APP. II PHB
do	5		Major J.A. LEAH assumed command. Relief by 2/4 GLOSTERS complete 3.35 pm. A Coy in Posts HOUGOMONT PICANTIN DEAD END LEVANTIE. E.	APP. 3 PHB
LEVANTIE	6		Working parties. Draft of 73 arrived.	PHB
"	7		do Preliminary order re move received	App. 4 PHB
ROBERMETZ	8 9		do Move to ROBERMETZ. All men except snipers in billets by 3 pm.	App 5 PHB
	9 10		Cleaning up Draft of 4 O/R received.	PHB
	11		Training. LE SART range	PHB
	12		Training Practice in Attack.	PHB
	13		do	PHB
	14		do	PHB
	15		do	PHB
	16		do . Orders re move to BOUT DEVILLE	App 6 PHB
	17		Move to BOUT DEVILLE F.G.C.M. 2181 Pte MORGAN	App 7 PHB

T2134. Wt. W708–776. 500000. 4/15. Sir J. C. & S.

Page 2

Instructions regarding War Diaries and Intelligence Summaries are contained in F. S. Regs., Part II. and the Staff Manual respectively. Title pages will be prepared in manuscript.

WAR DIARY
or
~~INTELLIGENCE SUMMARY.~~
(Erase heading not required.)

2/6 BN. GLOUCESTERSHIRE REGT.

Army Form C. 2118.

Place	Date	Hour	Summary of Events and Information	Remarks and references to Appendices
1916	1916			
BOUT DEVILLE	18 Aug		Relief of 13 YORKS & LANCS. POSTS taken over at CURZON, Pt ARTHUR & HILLS	App. 8 PHB
Trenches N. NEUVE CHAPELLE	19 "		Trenches - v. quiet	PHB
	20 "		do - do	PHB
	21.		do - do	PHB
	22		Relief by 2/4 GLOSTERS. Reserve billets at CROIX BARBEE	App 9 PHB
CROIX BARBEE	23		Working Parties. Training of men available.	PHB
	24		do do	PHB
	25		do do	PHB
	26		Relief of 2/7 WARWICKS in MOATED GRANGE sector.	App 10 PHB
Trenches N. MOATED GRANGE	27		Trenches - quiet.	PHB
	28		do - quiet.	PHB
	29		do - do. 2Lieut. WARWICK rejoined. 2LIEUT FOSTER joined	PHB
	30		do - do	PHB
	31		do Orders re move (relief by 2/4 GLOSTERS). 2Lieut Butler & 2Lieut MAY joined.	App 11 PHB

J. G. Reid
1/9/16
Lieut-Col.
Commdg. 2/6 Glosters

T2134. Wt. W708—776. 500000. 4/15. Sir J. C. & S.

Appendix I

2/6th Battalion The Gloucestershire Regiment.

SECRET.

ORDERS BY MAJOR A.D.BARTLEET, COMMANDING.

1. The 2/6th Bn. Gloster Regt., will relieve the 2/4th Bn. Gloster Regt., in left sub-section on August 1st 1916.

2. "A" Company 2/6th Glos. will relieve "B" Company 2/4th Glosters.
   "B" " " " " "C" " "
   "C" " " " " "D" " "
   "D" " " " " "A" " "

3. The leading section of "D" Company will leave LAVENTIE at 4 a.m. proceeding via PICANTIN AVENUE. The leading section of "C" Company in RESERVE LINE off RIFLEMANS AVENUE will leave at 4.30 a.m., and that in RESERVE LINE off PICANTIN at same time.
   The leading section of "B" Company will leave LAVENTIE at 5.30 a.m. proceeding via GREAT NORTH ROAD and RIFLEMAN.

4. Headquarter Staff will leave LAVENTIE at 8.45 a.m. and/ proceed to RED HOUSE.

5. Lewis Gun Section will leave LAVENTIE at 9.30 a.m. proceeding via GREAT NORTH ROAD and RIFLEMAN.

6. Company Signallers will proceed with ther Companies and will take over at 10. 0 a.m.

7. "D" Company will furnish a garrison of 1 N.C.O. and 3 Men for A1 POST.

8. Stores in POSTS now occupied by "C" Company will be checked and handed over to "D" Company of the 2/4th Bn. Gloster Regt., at 5.30 p.m. this day, 31st July 1916.

9. Guard in LAVENTIE EAST and FORK ROAD will be relieved about noon and will rejoin their Companies in the Line.

10. After relief is completed, GREAT NORTH ROAD and RIFLEMANS AVENUE will be used for UP traffic, and PICANTIN for DOWN traffic, except in the case of an attack, when PICANTIN will be used for both: BOND STREET will also be used for DOWN traffic.

11. When relief is completed each Company will wire "NO CONDIDATES".

12. Arrangements for water will be carried out as before.

13. The rations for to-morrow (except breakfast) will be at GREAT NORTHERN RAIL BASE to-night at 9.30 p.m. O.C. "C" Company will detail 1 N.C.O. and 2 Men to take charge at rail head, and hand/ over to parties from Companies as the relief is complete.
    From August 1st 2 Men per Company will proceed to GREAT NORTHERN RAIL BASE to take charge of rations.
    Rations will be drawn from RAIL HEAD under Company arrangements.

14. Disposition and "Taking Over" certificates to be at Battalion Headquarters by 2 p.m.

15. Requisitions for R.E. Stores, Work Reports, and Tactical Progress Reports to be at Battalion Headquarters by 6.30 a.m. daily: (Headquarter Orderly will be at Junction PICANTIN - TILLELOY Roads at 6 a.m., to received these.).
    SITUATION Reports will be sent by 'phone to reach Battalion Headquarters by 3 a.m. and 3 p.m. daily.
    CASUALTY Reports to be sent by Runner to reach Battalion Headquarters by 12 noon daily.

SECRET. APPENDIX 2.

183rd. BRIGADE ORDER NO. 33. COPY 4.

1. 4th. Glosters will relieve 6th. Glosters. in Left Sub-Section on August 5th, commencing at 12 noon. The relief must be by small parties. All details to be arranged by C.O's concerned.

2. 8th. Worcesters will relieve 7th. Worcesters in Right Sib-Section on August 5th, commencing at 6a.m. The relief will be by small parties. All details to be arranged by C.O's concerned.

3. Lewis Guns and Signallers of 4th. Glosters will relieve those of 6th. Glosters at 9a.m.

4. Lewis Guns and Signallers of 8th. Worcesters will relieve those of 7th. Worcesters at 12 noon.

5. 1 Officer and 1 N.C.O. per Company will proceed to the Trenches on the 4th. inst., to be shewn exactly what work is being done, and what needs immediate attention.

6. Distribution Return will be rendered by noon August 6th.

7. Handing Over and Taking over Certificates to Staff Captain by 9a.m. August 6th.

8. No relief will take place in Machine Gun Company and Trench Mortar Battery on August 5th.

9. All Units will report completion of relief to Brigade Headquarters.

(Signed) M.M. Parry Jones. Capt.

Bde. Major 183rd. Infantry Brigade.

SECRET. *Appendix 3*

2/6th. Battalion The Gloucestershire Regiment.

ORDERS BY MAJOR A.D.BARTLEET - COMMANDING. 4. 8. 1916.

1. The Battalion willbe relieved by the 2/4th. Glosters to-morrow August 5th. 1916.

2. "A" Company 2/6th. Glosters will be relieved by "B" Company 2/4th. Glosters.
"B" Company 2/6th. Glosters will be relieved by "C" Company 2/4th Glosters.

"C" Company " " " " " " "D" " "
"D" " " " " " " " "A" " "

3. Left and Left Centre Companies will be relieved about 12.30 p.m.
Right Centre Company " " " " 2p.m.
Right Company " " " " 3.30p.m.

4. Headquarters Signallers will be relieved at 9a.m.
Lewis Gunners and Snipers will be relieved at 9.30a.m.

5. "A" Company and 2 Lewis Guns will garrison Posts vacated by "D" Company, 2/4th. Glosters, viz:- 1 Platoon PICANTIN, 2 Platoons DEAD END, 1 Platoon HOUGOMONT.

6. "B" Company will find a Guard of 1 N.C.O. and 3 men, each for LAVENTIE EAST and FORK ROAD, to relieve 2/4th. Glosters, about 3.30p.m.

7. When relieved each Company will return to billets ("A" Company to Posts) by PICANTIN.

8. Officer or N.C.O. with leading Section will report Relief complete at RED HOUSE.

9. Unconsumed portion of days rations to be carried on the men.

10. Handing over certificates and List of Stores to be at Battalion Headquarters LAVENTIE by 6p.m.

11. MESS CART will be at RED HOUSE at 3p.m.

(Signed) P.H.BECK. Captain.

A/Adjutant. 2/6th. Bn. Gloster Regiment.

SECRET. APPENDIX 4.

Copy No. 6.

183rd. BRIGADE PRELIMINARY ORDER.

7. 8. 1916.

1. 184th. Infantry Brigade will relieve 183rd. Infantry Brigade in the FAUQUISSART Section on Wednesday August 9th.

2. The 2nd. Bucks will relieve 8th. Worcesters in the Right Sub-Section. 8th. Worcesters will go into Billets vacated by the 5tn. Glosters in LA GORGUE.

3. 4th. Oxfords will relieve the 4th. Glosters in the Left Sub-Section. 4th. Glosters will go into Billets vacated by the 4th. Berks in LA GORGUE.

4. 5th. Glosters will go into Billets at present occupied by the 7th. Worcesters (Right Battalion in Reserve). 7th. Worcesters will go into Billets vacated by the 2nd. Bucks at GRAND PACAUT, Sheet 36A - K.35.d.Central.

5. 4th. Berks will go into Billets at present occupied by the 6th. Glosters (Left Battalion in Reserve). 6th. Glosters will go into Billets vacated by 4th. Oxfords in ROBERMETZ - Sheet 36A - K.24.East Central.

6. 183rd. L.T.M.Battery will be relieved by 184th. L.T.M. Battery, and will go into Billets vacated by the. at LA GORGUE.

7. 183rd. Machine Gun Company will be relieved by 184th. Machine Gun Company , and will go into Billets vacated at LESTREM.

8. All Units will send an advanced Billeting Party, and will leave behind one Officer and one N.C.O. per Company. (This includes M.G. Company and L.T.M.Battery), to hand over Billets and make sure all is in order as regards Billet Stores etc.

9. Further detailed Orders as regards times etc., will be issued shortly.

(Signed) M.M.Parry Jones. Capt.

Bde. Major. 183rd. Infantry Brigade.

Appendix 5.

Operation Order No. 1 by Major F.A.Leah, O.C. 2/6th Glos. Regt.

Ref. Map.
Sheet 36A.

In the Field.
8.8.16.

1. RELIEF.

The 4th Berks. will relieve 2/6th Glosters to-morrow 9th inst., commencing 9.30 a.m. The 2/6th Glosters will go into billets vacated by 4th Oxfords at ROBERMETZ (sheet 36A K.24.d. central)

2. BILLETTING.

Captain Fisher (mounted), Lieut. Baron, and 1 N.C.O. per Company (on bicycles), will parade at Orderly Room at 9.0 a.m. and proceed to ROBERMETZ as billetting party.

Captain Fisher will see that no billets are taken over which are not clean, and will also take over the transport lines of 4th Berks, and any Training Ground which may be in the vicinity

The Orderly Officer and 1 N.C.O. per Company will remain behind at LAVENTIE and hand over all billets at present occupied, to the 4th Berks Regt: the usual certificate of cleanliness being obtained.

3. STARTING POINT.

LAVENTIE Level Crossing.

4. ROUTE.

LA GORGUE: L.28.d.Central: L.27.d.2.5: K.30.d.3.3:
K.24.c.9.3, where Billetting Party will meet incoming Companies and lead them to their billets.

5. ORDER OF MARCH.

Companies march as under : "B" Company.
"C" "
"D" "
"A" "

Marching by Companies at 100 yards intervals.

Lewis Gunners, Signallers, Pioneers, Police, and Snipers, will march as a Company, and follow "A" Company.

The head of "B" Company will pass the Starting Point at 8.30 a.m. Cookers will accompany their Companies. All Details will rejoin their Companies for meals.

6. RATIONS.

Rations will be drawn to-day as usual. Meat will be cut up and placed in the Cooker, and dinners served on arrival at ROBERMETZ.

7. LEWIS GUNS.

Lewis Gun Officer will arrange with Transport Officer as to the carriage of Lewis Guns.

8. POSTS & KEEPS.

The O.C. "A" Company will render at once to the Orderly Room a return of all Trench Stores etc., in the various Keeps. He will also obtain a receipt from the incoming Unit.

9. RELIEF.

Completion of relief to be reported to present Battn. Headqrs. and arrival in billets to be reported to Battn. Headqrs ROBERMETZ.

(Sd). P.H.BECK Captain.
A/Adjutant, 2/6th Glosters.

10. Officers' Kits and Mess Boxes should be ready at their respective Company Headqrs. at 8.30 a.m. O.C. "A" Company will arrange for his Kits and Mess Box to be ready at 9.30 a.m. p The Transport Officer will arrange for a limber to collect these.

11. MARCH DISCIPLINE.

The strictest attention must be paid to March Discipline. The 2 top buttons of the tunic will be undone. Companies must keep to the right of the road, and the fours be correctly covered off. The Companies must march closed up.

Nothing will be carried on the Cookers except the Cook's pack.

Mess tins will be either carried in the pack, or strapped underneath the pack, and not left dangling from the valise or haversack. Excessive drinking on the march is forbidden.

No N.C.O. or man will be allowed to fall out without a pass signed by an Officer. Falling out states to be rendered at once on arrival in billets. Steel helmets will not be worn.

12. Prior to leaving billets Companies should be paraded outside at least half an hour before marching off, and a fatigue party detailed to see that no waste paper or food, or other refuse is lying about.

(Sd). P.H.BECK Captain.

A/Adjutant, 2/6th Glosters.

SECRET. APPENDIX 6.

No. 3.

BRIGADE OPERATION ORDER NO. 35.

1. 2/6 Glosters will move into Billets at BOUT DEVILLE R.24.a.4.8. Sheet 36a to-morrow Thursday 17th instant. They will leave ROBERMETZ at2.30 p.m.

2. 2/7 Worcesters will move into Billets at CROIX BARBEE Sheet 36 M.26.c.8.3. to-morrow Thursday 17th instant. They will leave GRAND PACAUT at 2.30 p.m.

3. The usual billetting parties will be sent by both units in advance to arrange billets. They will report to Staff Captain at Brigade Headquarters at 10 a.m. for instructions re Billets.

4. Transport of 6th Glosters will be billeted at M.20.d.0.0. Transport of 7th Worcesters will be billetted at R.30.c.5.9.

5. On arrival each Battalion will send an Orderly to 94th Brigade Headquarters at R.29.d.7.8. and will report through that Brigade completion of move.
The Orderlies will remain at Headquarters 94th Brigade for the purpose of communication with this Brigade.

6. Further orders will follow as regards taking over the line.

M.M. Parry Jones Captain.
Brigade Major 183rd Inf. Brigade.

APPENDIX 7.

PROVISIONAL. FURTHER ORDERS MAY BE ISSUED LATER.

2/6th Battalion Gloucester Regiment.

Operation Orders No. 3. 16.8.1916.

In the Field.

Ref. Sheet 36a or
Bethune Combined.

1. MOVE. The 2/6th Glosters will move into billets at BOUT DEVILLE R.24.a.4.8. to-morrow, Thursday 17th inst.,

2. ORDER OF MARCH. The Battalion will parade at 2 p.m. in order of "A", "B", "C", "D". Starting Point the road Junction opposite Lewis Gun Billet. Headqr. Signallers, Pioneers, Lewis Gunners, will follow "D" Company.

3. BILLETING PARTY. This will consist of Lieut. Baron, 1 N.C.O. per Company, and the Armr. Staff Serjeant Stanley (for Headqrs.) on bicycles. They will parade at Battalion Headqrs. at 9 a.m., and report to the Staff Captain at Brigade Headquarters, LA GORGUE, at 10 a.m., for instructions re billeting.

4. TRANSPORT. The Transport will be billeted at M.20.d.0.0.

5. All Officers' Mess Boxes, and Kits, to be at Quartermaster's Stores at 1 p.m., and the Transport Officer will arrange for the collecting of same.

6. COMMUNICATION. On arrival in billets one orderly will be sent from Battn. Headqrs. to 94th Brigade Headqrs. at R.29.d.7.8., and report to that Brigade the completion of the move. This orderly will remain with the Headqrs. of the 94th Brigade for the purpose of communication with the 183rd Brigade.

7. MEALS. Dinners at 12 noon. Tea to be made on the way and served on arrival in billets.

8. BILLETS. Billets to be left scrupulously clean, and the Orderly Officer will remain behind to hand over all Stores left behind, and to obtain a certificate of cleanliness as to billets.

9. ROUTE. The Battalion will march as a battalion, via BEAUPRE - LESTREM ROAD and FOSSE. East of the River LAWE, Companies will shake out and march by Platoons at 100 yards distance.

10. MARCH DISCIPLINE. The strictest attention must be paid to all Battalion Orders with reference to March Discipline. Men must not fall out. Half of the servants will be with their Companies. Cooks and all Details will be properly dressed.

(Signed) P.H.BECK Captain.

A/Adjutant, 2/6th Glosters.

SECRET. 2/6th. BATTALION THE GLOUCESTERSHIRE REGIMENT. Appendix 8

OPERATION ORDERS NO. 4 BY MAJOR F.A. LEAH COMMANDING.

IN THE FIELD. 17. 8. 1916.

REFERENCE:- BETHUNE(COMBINED)AND BRIGADE TRENCH MAP.

1. The 2/6th. Bn. Gloster Regiment will relieve the 13th. Yorks and Lancs. in NEUVE CHAPPELLE Sub Sector (Left).
   Relief to be completed by 6p.m.

2. ORDER OF RELIEF. Companies will take over from corresponding Companies of the 13th. Yorks and Lancs. Signallers. Lewis Gunners, and Snipers will parade at 9.30a.m. outside Battalion Orderly Room, also parties detailed from "D" Company to take over HILLS and PORT ARTHUR REDOUBTS. Guides to meet these parties will be at EUSTON POST M.33.b.9.9. at 10.30a.m.

3. One Officer and one N.C.O. per Company will leave Billets for purpose of taking over Trench Stores at 9.30a.m. Guides for ~~taking over~~ other Companies as under:-
   "C" Company - Guides will meet Company at CROIX ROUGE M.27.b.0.7. at 2.30p.m. Company to enter via BALUCHI Trench.
   "A" Company.) Guides at EUSTON POST M.33.b.9.9. at
   "B" Company.) 2.30.p.m.
   "D" Company.)

4. ORDER OF MARCH. "C" Company) Connecting Files to be
   "A" Company.) arranged so that Companies do
   "B" Company.) not close up.
   "D" Company.)
   Companies will move by Platoons at a 100 yards distance; East of line N and S through RICHBOURG and CROIX BARBEE, Companies will move by Sections at a 100 yards distance.

5. STORES. Lists of Maps, Trench Stores & c., to reach Battalion Headquarters by 6p.m.

6. LEWIS GUNS. The Transport Officer will arrange for Limbers to carry Lewis Guns and also Signalling and Snipers Equipment. They will proceed as far as the SHRINE at M.32.d.6.8.

7. COMPLETION OF RELIEF. Completion of Relief is to be reported by Runner. Code for Completion "PUSSYS IN THE WELL".

8. GUIDE FOR HEADQUARTERS. Guide for Headquarters willbbe at EUSTON POST at 3.15p.m.

9. GARRISON FOR CURZON POST. Pioneers, Officers Servants, Police & c., will furnish Garrison for CURZON POST - Strength - One Platoon.

10. RETURNS. O.C. Companies will render to Battalion Orderly Room by 8p.m. a rough Sketch, also Trench Strength Return, shewing total strength, men available for Fire Bays, men at Battalion Headquarters, details for Company Employ in Trenches, Snipers, Lewis Gunners & c., men away from the Battalion, and by 6pm. the 19th. inst., a Scheme of Defence; the question of meeting hostile raids by local counter attack will always be kept in view.
    Situation Reports - 3a.m. and 3p.m.
    Casualty Reports - 12 noon.
    R.E.Stores , Tactical Progress Report and Ammunition Indent to reach Battalion Headquarters - 6.30a.m.

11. TRENCH KITS ETC. Officers Trench Kits and Mess Boxes to be at Quarter Master Stores by 1 p.m. Officers need not carry packs, but Subaltern Officers should carry rifles if available.

(Signed) P.H.BECK. Captain.

A/Adjutant. 2/6th. Battalion Gloucester Regiment.

Appendix 9

2/6th Battalion Gloster Regiment.

SECRET.

OPERATION ORDER NO. 6 BY MAJOR F.A.LEAH. COMMANDING.

Ref. BETHUNE (Combined)sheet
and BRIGADE TRENCH MAP.

In the Field
21. 8. 1916.

1. RELIEF. (a) The 2/4th. Bn. Gloster Regt., will relieve the 2/6th. Bn. Gloster Regt., in NEUVE CHAPELLE Section (Left Sub-Sector) to-morrow, August 22nd. 1916, commencing at 12 noon. The Relief will be in small-parties.

(b) The 2/6th. Bn. Gloster Regt., will go into Billets vacated by the 2/4th. Bn. Gloster Regt., at CROIX BARBEE (RUE DU PUITS) and become Left Battalion in Reserve.

2. BILLETS. Lieut. S.T.BARON and 1 N.C.O. per Company will parade at Battalion Orderly Room to-morrow at 9a.m. and proceed to CROIX BARBEE for the purpose of taking over Billets.

3. LEWIS GUNS ETC. Lewis Guns, Signallers, and Snipers etc., will be relieved by 12 noon. Three Lewis Gun Teams relieved in front line will take over in HILLS and PORT ARTHUR.

4. ORDER OF RELIEF. "C" Coy. 4th. Glosters relieve "C" Company 6th. Glosters.
"D" Company 4th. Glosters relieve "B" Company 6th. Glosters.
"B" Company 4th. Glosters relieve "A" Company 6th. Glosters.
"A" Company 4th. Glosters relieve "D" Company 6th. Glosters.

SHEET 2.

No. 5.

GUIDES. (a) Guides for Lewis Gunners, Signallers, & Snipers, will be at EUSTON POST (M.34.a.1.8.) at 9 a.m.
Guides for HILLS & PORT ARTHUR at the same place and at the same time.
(b) Company guides as under:-
"C" Company at BALUCHI TRENCH (M34.b.2.5) at 12.30 p.m.
"B" Company at EUSTON POST - 1 p.m.
"A" " " " " = 1.15 p.m.
"D" " " " " = 1.30 p.m.
Bn. H.Q. " " " = 2 p.m.
4 Guides per Company to be provided.
(c) 1 Officer and 1 N.C.O. per Company of 4th Glosters will arrive during the morning for the purpose of taking over Stores.
Guides need not be provided.

6. POSTS. "D" Company will provide Garrisons for the undermentioned Posts:-
LORETTO (M.33.b.2.5.)
2 Sections, 1 Vickers Gun.
EUSTON.- 2 Sections, 1 Vickers and 1 Lewis Gun.
RUE DU PUITS. 1 N.C.O. and 3 Men.
CROIX BARBEE. 1 N.C.O. and 3 Men.

7. CODE. Code for completion of relief "PETROL TINS", to present H.Qrs. On arrival in Billets report to Bn. H.Qrs. RUE DU PUITS.

8. STORES. List of Stores handed over to 2/4th Glosters to be sent to Bn. Orderly Room (present Bn. H.Qrs.) by 2 p.m.
List of Stores taken over from 2/4th Glosters to be at new H.Qrs. (RUE DU PUITS) by 6 p.m.

SHEET 3.

9. TRAFFIC ORDER. E. of R. LAWE troops will move by Platoons at 100 yds. distance. E. of a line N. & S. through RICHEBOURG and CROIX BARBEE by Sections at 100 yds. distance.

10. BILLETS. Lieut. S.T.Baron will arrange for Company Guides to be at Cross Roads at Croix Barbee (M.26.c.7.3.) to meet incoming Companies.

11. GUIDES. Guides for Posts furnished by "D" Company will be found by 2/4th Glosters and will be at EUSTON POST at 5 p.m.

12. OFFICERS' KITS & MESS BXS. Transport Officer will arrange to have a limber at THE SHRINE at 3 p.m.

13. LEWIS GUNS. Transport Officer will arrange to have a limber at THE SHRINE at 12 noon.

(Signed) P.H.BECK Capt.
A/Adjutant, 2/6th Glosters.

Secret

Appendix 10

2/6th Battalion Gloucester Regiment.

Operation Order No. by LIEUT. COL. F.A.LEAH, O. Cmdg.

2/6th Battalion Gloucester Regiment.

Ref. BETHUNE Cbd. Sheet.
Sheet 36A & Bd:.Trench
Map Area J.

In the Field.
25.8.1916.

1. RELIEF. The 6th Gloucesters will relieve the 7th Warwicks in the Left Subsection (MOATED GRANGE Section) to-morrow 26th inst., Relief to be complete by 6.p.m.

2. TRANSPORT. Transport will take over Lines of 7th Warwicks at L.35.c.3.2.

3. BILLETS. Lieut. BARON and 1 N.C.O. per Coy. will remain behind to hand over Billets, Stores & Posts, Keeps etc., to incoming Battalion 13th Yorks. & Lancs. Billets to be left as clean as possible. Yorks. & Lancs. will arrive at 9.30 a.m.

4. ORDER OF RELIEF.
"C" Company will relieve "B" Company (Left).
"B" " " " "A" " (Centre).
"D" " " " "C" & "D" Companies (Right).
"A" " " take over Posts, and Keeps (less WINCHESTER POST which will be garrisoned by Police, Pioneers etc.,), the balance going into Reserve Line.

5. ROUTE. (The relief will be by Sections at 100^x distance. The RUE DU BACQUEROT will not be used by the Left Battn. between ROUGE CROIX & MIN. ST., Companies will proceed by M.20.a.4.5 - PONT DU HEM & LA FLINQUE.

6. GUIDES. Guides for Lewis Gunners, Signallers, Snipers, & Post & Keepers (in order mentioned for marching off) will be at LA FLINQUE at 10 a.m.
Guides for Companies as under:-
"C" Company at WINCHESTER RD. at 2 p.m.
"B" " " " " " 2.15 p.m.
Stn. TILLELOY. "D" " " ~~MIN. ST.~~ at 1.45 p.m.
"A" " " WINCHESTER RD. at 2.30 p.m.

7. WORK. O.Cs. Coys. will take particular care to see that on taking over they receive all particulars as to work in hand in Front Line & Reserve.

8. CODE ON COMPLETION. Will be "HARRY TATE".

9. WATER. The M.O. will arrange for water carts to be brought up at dusk.

10. ADVANCE PARTY. 1 Officer per Coy. & 1 N.C.O. per Coy. will proceed to the Trenches in the morning for the purpose of taking over Stores. The Bombing Officer will also accompany this party.

11. LEWIS GUNS. The Transport Officer will have a limber at Bn. Headqrs. at 8 a.m. for conveying Lewis Guns. Officers' Trench Kits, & Mess Boxes, will be at Bn. H.Q. by 1 p.m. The Transport Officer will arrange for these to be taken up to the Trenches. Officers' Valises to be at the Canteen by 12 mid-day.

(Signed) P.H.BECK Captain.
A/Adjutant, 2/6th Glosters.

P.T.O.

Operation Orders. No. (Continued).

12. RETURNS TO Bn. H.Q. (c) O.Cs. Coys., O.C. Lewis Guns, to render a disposition return (rough sketch) as soon as possible.
(b) Defence Scheme to be submitted 24 hours after relief.
(c) List of Stores taken over by 6 p.m.

13. ORDERLY OFFICER. LIEUT. BARON will obtain a receipt for all Stores taken over, and also a certificate as to cleanliness of Billets.

14. WORKING PARTY. The O.C. "A" Coy. will detail 1 N.C.O. and 25 men as a permanent R.E. working party to be billetted at M.9.b.3.0.
The Q.M. will ration this party. This party will report to Bde. H.Q. to Staff Captain at 6 p.m. 26th inst.

15. CARE OF FEET. Platoon Commanders must see that the men take care of their feet.
Boots and Socks must be taken off daily, and if possible the feet washed.

(Signed) F.H.BECK Captain.
A/Adjutant, 2/6th Gloucesters.

Appendix 11

SECRET.

Copy No. 7.

30.8.1916.

183rd BRIGADE ORDER No. 39.

---

1. 4th Glosters will relieve 6th GLOSTERS in the Left Subsection (MOATED GRANGE SECTION) on September 1st, commencing at 2 p.m.
   Relief of Posts, and all other details to be arranged by C.Os. concerned. 6th GLOSTERS will take over Billets vacated by 8th WORCESTERS South of H.7.d.7.5.

2. 8th WORCESTERS will relieve 7th WORCESTERS in the Right Sub-Section (MOATED GRANGE SECTION) on September 1st commencing 9 a.m. Relief of Posts and all other details to be arranged by C.Os. concerned. 7th WORCESTERS will take over Billets vacated by 4th GLOSTERS.

3. Lewis Guns & Signallers in both cases will be relieved by 12 noon September 1st.

4. No relief will take place in Machine Gun Coy or Light Trench Mortar Battery on September 1st.

5. Para. 19 of 61st Division Standing Orders will be complied with the day before relief.

6. Distribution Return by 12 noon September 2nd.

7. Handing-Over and Taking-Over Certificates to the Staff Captain by 9 a.m. September 2nd.

8. Units will report completion of relief to Brigade H.Q. Code:- "Quite enough, thanks".

(Signed) H.T.Harris, Captain.
for Brigade Major, 183rd Infantry Brigade.

Confidential

Vol 5

War Diary

of

2/6th Bn. Gloster Regiment

From 1. 9. 1916 To 30. 9. 1916.

Volume #. 5

Page I

Instructions regarding War Diaries and Intelligence Summaries are contained in F. S. Regs., Part II. and the Staff Manual respectively. Title pages will be prepared in manuscript.

WAR DIARY 2/6 Bn. GLOUCESTERSHIRE REGT.

or

~~INTELLIGENCE SUMMARY.~~

(Erase heading not required.)

Army Form C. 2118.

Place	Date	Hour	Summary of Events and Information	Remarks and references to Appendices
1916	1916			
Trenches	Apl 1		Relief by 7/4 Glosters. Completed 4.15 p.m. Billets RIEZ BAILLEUL	APP I PHB
RIEZ BAILLEUL	2		Baths & cleaning up	PHB
	3		Working parties	PHB
	4		Holiday & Sports	PHB
	5		Working parties	PHB
	6		do & Training. Ordered relieving 7/4 GLOSTERS	PHB
MOATED GRANGE	7		Relief of 7/4 GLOSTERS - patrols to inspect ground for raid	APP 2. PHB
do	8		Trenches - quiet - ~~patrols to inspect ground for raid~~	
do			Raid of 2 parties - object to capture prisoner - one party of Lieut R. GATEY & 50 O.R. on right, one party of Lieut. HUGHES-GAMES ~~an~~ & 20 O.R. on left, left trenches at 8.30 p.m. Of right party about 6 entered German trenches, captured German but had to abandon him after killing him since wire was too thick to get him across. Other party did not get through wire but lay in wait for E. patrol without success. Casualties officers. 2 wounded O.R. 1 killed 5 wounded	PHB

T2134. Wt. W708—776. 500000. 4/15. Sir J. C. & S.

Page 2.

Instructions regarding War Diaries and Intelligence Summaries are contained in F. S. Regs., Part II. and the Staff Manual respectively. Title pages will be prepared in manuscript.

WAR DIARY
or ~~INTELLIGENCE SUMMARY~~. of 2/6 Bn. GLOUCESTERSHIRE REGT.

(Erase heading not required.)

Army Form C. 2118.

Place	Date	Hour	Summary of Events and Information	Remarks and references to Appendices
	1916			
MOATED GRANGE	Sept 9		Trenches - quiet -	PHB
	10		do. Further attempt to capture German patrol by Lieut. HUGHES-GAMES + 20 O.R. Bangalore torpedo exploded under German wire about 1.40 am.	PHB
	11		Relief by 1/4 Oxf Bucks Bn. Billets at LA GORGUE.	APP 3 PHB
LA GORGUE	12		Cleaning + interior economy	PHB
	13		Baths, training, working parties.	PHB
	14		Training	PHB
	15		do	PHB
	16		Relief of 18th Bn. D.L.I. in NEUVE CHAPELLE SECTOR.	APP 4 PHB
NEUVE CHAPELLE	17		Trenches. quiet	PHB
	18		do	PHB
	19		do Small raid attempted. Bangalore did not completely cut wire.	PHB
	20		Relief by 1/4 GLOSTERS. Billets at BOUT DEVILLE. 1 NCO + 30 OR in RUE DE PUITS post.	APP 5 PHB
BOUT DEVILLE	21		Interior economy - Cleaning &c.	PHB

T2134. Wt. W708—776. 500000. 4/15. Sir J. C. & S.

Army Form C. 2118.

Instructions regarding War Diaries and Intelligence Summaries are contained in F. S. Regs., Part II. and the Staff Manual respectively. Title pages will be prepared in manuscript.

WAR DIARY 2/6 Bn. GLOUCESTERSHIRE REGT.
or
~~INTELLIGENCE SUMMARY~~.

(*Erase heading not required.*)

Place	Date	Hour	Summary of Events and Information	Remarks and references to Appendices
	1916			
BOUTDEVILLE	Sept 22		Baths & Training. Working parties	PHB
do	23		Training. Working Parties.	PHB
do	24		do do & Church Parade	PHB
do	25		do do	PHB
do	26		Relief of 2/4 GLOSTERS in NEUVE CHAPELLE Sector ~~APP~~	APP 6 PHB
NEUVE CHAPELLE SECT	27		Trenches. Quiet except for H.T.M. at head of CHATEAU TRENCH.	PHB
do	28		do do	PHB
do	29		do do	PHB
do	30		do do	PHB

F. A. Rady [?] Lt. Col. Commdg.
1/10/16 2/6 Bn. Gloucestershire Regt

T2134. Wt. W708—776. 500000. 4/15. Sir J. C. & S.

VERY SECRET.

Appendix I

OPERATION ORDER NO. 7.

By Lieut. Colonel F. A. LEAH, Officer Commanding The 2/6th Battalion The Gloucestershire Regiment.

Ref. Bde. Trench Map. & BETHUNE Combined.

In the Field.
31. 8. 1916.

1. RELIEF.
(a) The 4th Glosters will relieve the 6th Glosters in the Left Sub-Section (MOATED GRANGE Section) on September 1st commencing at 2 p.m.
(b) The 6th Glosters will take over billets vacated by 8th Worcesters South of M.7.d.7.5.
(c) Lewis Guns and Signallers will be relieved by 12 noon.

2. BILLETS. Lieut. S.T.BARON and 1 N.C.O. per Company will parade at Battalion Orderly Room at 8 a.m. and proceed to RIEZ BAILLEUL for the purpose of taking over Billets.

3. GUIDES. Guides for Lewis Gunners, Signallers, Snipers, H.Q. Bombers (DREADNOUGHT POST), WINCHESTER and TILLELOY N. POSTS to be at WINCHESTER RD. M.23a. at 10 a.m. COMPANY GUIDES as under:-

"D" Company at TILLELOY S. at 2.30 p.m.
"C" " " WINCHESTER ROAD at 3 p.m.
"B" " " " " " 2.30 p.m.
Battn. Hdqrs. at " " " 3.15 p.m.

4. CODE ON COMPLETION. Code on completion will be "NUFF" to present Battn. Hdqrs.

5. STORES. All Stores, Ammunition, Bombs, Tools, etc., to be checked as soon as possible ready for handing over. List of Stores handed over to be at Battn. Orderly Room by 1 p.m.

6. TRANSPORT.
(a) Transport Lines will not be changed.
(b) The Transport Officer will arrange to have Limbers for Lewis Guns, Signalling Equip-ment, at EPINETTE FARM at 11 a.m.
(c) Officers' trench kits and mess boxes to be at EPINETTE FARM at 2 p.m. Transport Officer to arrange for carriage of same.

7. ROUTE.
(a) ROUTE TO BILLETS: LA FLINQUE - PONT DU HEM.
(b) "D" Company - M.22.c.2.5. - PONT DU HEM.
(c) "B" Company will leave the Trenches through MIN STREET.

8. GUIDES. Guides for Billets to meet incoming Companies at M.20.central.
Officers Commanding Companies to report arrival in Billets to Battn. Headqrs.

(Signed) P.H.BECK Captain.
A/Adjutant, 2/6th Battn. Gloster Regiment.

VERY SECRET.   Appendix 2

Operation Order No. 8 by Lieut. Col. F. A. Leah,

Commanding 2/6th Battalion Gloucestershire Regt.

Ref: BETHUNE Combined
Sheet 36A, and
Brigade Trench Map.   6.9.1916.

1. RELIEF. The 6th Glosters will relieve the 4th Glosters in the Left Sub-section (MOATED GRANGE), to-morrow 7th September starting at 9 a.m.

2. BILLETS. Lieut. S.T.Baron and 1 N.C.O. per Company will remain behind to hand over billets and stores to the 2/8th Worcesters. This Officer and the N.C.O. from each Company will be at the Orderly Room at at 9.30 a.m. to-morrow Sept. 7th.

3. ORDER OF RELIEF. "D" Coy. 2/6th Glosters will relieve "C" Coy. 2/4 Glosters on the Left. "B" Coy. 2/6th Glosters will relieve "A" Coy. 2/4th Glosters in the Centre. "A" Coy. 2/6th Glosters will relieve "D" Coy. 2/4 Glosters on the Right.
"C" Coy. will take over Posts and Keeps as under:-
WINCHESTER - 2 Platoons. GRANTS - ½ Platoon.
DREADNOUGHT - ½ Platoon. TILLELOY NORTH - 1 platoon.
ERITH POST M.34.d.0.8 will be garrisoned by 1 N.C.O. and 8 men, to be found by O.C. "D" Coy. Police and Pioneers will also be part of the garrison of WINCHESTER POST.

4. ROUTE. The relief will be by Sections at 100^x distance. Coys. and Sections will proceed via PONT DU HEM - LA FLINQUE.

5. GUIDES. Guides as under:-
At the bottom of WINCHESTER trench on RUE BACQUEROT:
Lewis Gunners 9 a.m. - Snipers 9.30 a.m. - Signallers 10 a.m. "D" Coy. 1.30 p.m. "B" Coy. 2 p.m. "A" Coy. 2.30 p.m. "C" Coy. 3 p.m.

6. WORK. O.Cs. Companies will take particular care to see that on taking over, they receive all particulars as to work in hand in front line and reserve.

7. CODE. Code on completion will be:- "What for please?".

8. WATER. The M.O. will arrange for water carts to be brought up at dusk. O.Cs. Companies and Sections will see that the men start with filled water bottles.

9. ADVANCE PARTY. 1 Officer and 1 N.C.O. per Company will proceed to the trenches in the morning, and arrive there not later than 11 a.m. for the purpose of taking over Stores. The Bombing Officer will accompany this party.

10. TRANSPORT. The Transport Officer will arrange to have transport as under:-
1. At 6.45 a.m. at Headqrs. to collect Lewis Guns, Signallers, and Snipers equipment.
2. Transport for Officers' kits for Q.M. Stores to call at billets at 4 p.m. (each package to be properly labelled with Officer's name - Company boxes with Company letter).

P.T.O.

3. For Stores and Officers' kits for Line, at Headqrs. at 2 p.m. (each Company will leave 2 Officers' servants behind - 1 to look after the packages for Q.M. Stores, and 1 to look after packages to go to the trenches. These servants will report to their Companies when their duties are finished.

11. RETURNS.
(a) O.Cs. Companies, Lewis Gunners, and Bombers, will render a Disposition Return by 8 p.m. Sept. 7th.
(b) Defence Scheme to be submitted 24 hours after relief.
(c) List of Stores taken over by 6 p.m. Sept. 7th.
(d) Tactical Progress, Ammunition Indents, R.E. Indents to be rendered by 6.30 a.m.
(e) Situation reports to be rendered at 2.45 a.m. and 2.45 p.m.
(f) Casualty Returns to be rendered noon daily.

12. CARE OF FEET.

O.Cs. Companies will see that the men take care of their feet. Boots and socks must be taken off daily in small numbers at a time and if possible the feet washed.

13. RATIONS. O.Cs. Companies, Snipers, Lewis Gunners, and Bombers, will each detail one N.C.O. to report at Headqrs. at 8.15 nightly to take charge of their rations.

14. MEALS. Dinners will be at noon to-morrow; the remainder of the days rations will be carried by the men.

15. GRENADE RIFLES. O.Cs. Companies will see that grenade rifles are taken to the trenches, and will be responsible for firing rifle grenades.

(Sd). P.H.BECK Captain.
A/Adjutant, 6th Glosters.

Appendix 3

VERY SECRET.

Operation Orders No. 9 by Lieut. Col. F.A.Leah, Commanding 2/6th Battn. Gloucester Regt.,

Map ref: Sheet 36 A and Sheet 36.

1. RELIEF. The 4th Oxfords and Bucks L.I. will relieve 6th Gloster Regt., in the Left Sub-section on Sept. 11th 1916: relief to be complete by 6 p.m.

6th Gloster Regt. will take over billets vacated by the 4th Bn. Royal Berks. at LA GORGUE.

"A" Coy. will be relieved by "C" Coy. 4th Oxford Regt.,
"B" " " " " " "D" " " " "
"D" " " " " " "A" " " " "
"C" " " " " " "B" " " " "

2. BILLETS. Lieut. S.T.Baron and 1 N.C.O. per Company will report at Battalion Headquarters at 9 a.m. to proceed to LA GORGUE for the purpose of taking over billets.

3. GUIDES. Guides for Lewis Guns, Snipers, and Signallers, and Medical Officer, will be at the junction of WINCHESTER Trench with RUE BACQUEROT at 12 noon.

"D" Company guide will be at the junction of WINCHESTER Trench - RUE BACQUEROT at 3 p.m.

The Right Company at 3.30 p.m.
The Centre " " 3.30 p.m.
Posts and Keeps and Battalion Headquarters at 3.45 p.m.
On relief O.C. "A" Company will leave trenches via MIN St.,

4. CODE. Code on completion: "CIGARETTES", to present Battalion Headquarters.

5. STORES. All Stores, Ammunition, Bombs, Tools, etc., to be checked as soon as possible, ready for handing over. One Officer and one N.C.O. per Company of the 4th Oxford Regt., will be in the trenches to take over about 12 noon.

List of Stores to be handed over to be at Battalion Orderly Room by 12 noon.

Lists signed by both Officers to be at Battalion Orderly Room by 4 p.m.

6. TRANSPORT. Transport Officer will arrange to have two limbers for Lewis Guns, Signalling, and Sniping equipment, at EPINETTE FARM at 1.30 p.m. Officers' trench kit and mess boxes to be at EPINETTE FARM at 3 p.m. Transport Officer to arrange carriage of same.

7. ROUTE. Companies will march to billets via LA FLINQUE Cross Roads - LE DRUMEZ - Road Junction G.32.a.2.½. Companies will march by sections at 100 yards as far as LA BASSEE Road.

8. GUIDES. Billeting Officer will arrange for guides to meet incoming Companies, and guide them to their billets. Officers Commanding Companies will report arrival in billets to Battalion Headquarters.

(Signed) P.H.BECK Captain.
A/Adjutant, 2/6th Glosters.

Appendix 4

VERY SECRET.

Operation Order No. 10 by Lieut. Colonel F.A.Leah,
Commanding 2/6th Battalion The Gloster Regiment.

16.9.1918.

1. RELIEF. The 6th Glosters will relieve 18th Bn. D.L.I. in Posts and Keeps in front line, and also the 18th Bn. West Yorks. in EUSTON POST - behind Right Fifteenth Street exclusive. Relief to be complete by 6 p.m. 16th inst.,

2. BILLETS. One Officer and One N.C.O. will remain behind to hand over Billets.

3. GUIDES. Guides for Snipers, Signallers, and Lewis Gunners, will be at entrance to BALUCHI Trench at 1 p.m.

Guides for	"A" Company	3 p.m.
" "	"D" "	3.15 p.m.
" "	"B" "	3.30 p.m.
" "	"C" "	3.30 p.m.

All at the head of BALUCHI Trench.

4. ORDER OF RELIEF. "B" Company will take over Posts as under :-

CHATEAU POST	1 N.C.O. and 19 O.R.
CHURCH "	1 N.C.O. and 6 O.R.
EUSTON "	1 Platoon.

CURZON POST will be garrisoned by Police, Pioneers, etc.

5. CODE ON COMPLETION. Code on completion will be "PERHAPS".

6. TRANSPORT. Officers' trench kits, and mess boxes to be at Battalion Headquarters by 2 p.m. Transport Officer to arrange limbers for the same. Officers' surplus kits must be clearly labelled, and sent to Quartermaster's Stores. Transport Officer to arrange carriage of same.

7. ORDER OF MARCH. Companies will move by Platoons at 100 yards distance as far as PONT du HEM: after that point by sections at 100 yards distance.

8. RETURNS. (a) O.Cs. Companies, Lewis Gunners, and Bombers, will render a Disposition Return by 9 p.m. 17th Sept.,
(b) Defence Scheme to be submitted 24 hours after relief.
(c) List of Stores taken over, by 7 p.m. Sept. 17th.
(d) Tactical Progress, Ammunition Indents, R.E. Indents, to be rendered by 6.30 a.m.
(e) Situation Reports to be rendered at 2.45 a.m. and 2.45 p.m.
(f) Casualty Returns to be rendered noon daily.

(Signed) P.H.BECK Captain.
A/Adjutant, 6 Glosters.

ADDENDUM.

ROUTE. Route will be: RIEZ BAILLEUL - CROIX BARBEE - SHRINE - - BALUCHI.

VERY SECRET.

Appendix 5

Operation Orders No. 11 by Lieut. Colonel F.A.Leah, Commanding 2/6th Gloster Regt.,

19.9.16.

1. RELIEF. The 4th Glosters will relieve the 6th Glosters in the Left Sub-section on Sept. 20th 1916: relief to be complete by 4 p.m.

6th Glosters will take over billets vacated by the 4th Glosters at BOUT DE VILLE, and also RUE DU PUITS POST.

"A" Company 6th Glosters will be relieved by "A" Company 4th Glos.

"D" " " " " " " "B" " " "

"D" Company 4th Glosters will be Right Company in "B" Line, and will take over CHURCH POST from "B" Company 6th Glosters.

"C" Company 4th Glosters will be Left Company in "B" Line, and will take over CHATEAU POST from "B" Company 6th Glosters.

2. BILLETS. 2nd Lieut. L.W.Just, 1 N.C.O. per Company, and 1 N.C.O. for Headquarters, will report at Battalion Headquarters at 9 a.m. to proceed to BOUT DE VILLE for the purpose of taking over billets.

3. GUIDES. Guides for Snipers, Lewis Gunners, and Signallers, will be on the LA BASSEE Road at EUSTON POST at 11 a.m. Guides for "A" Company 4th Glosters will be at EUSTON POST at 1.30 p.m. Guides for "B" Company 4th Glosters will be at EUSTON POST at 1.45 p.m. Guides for "C" Company 4th Glosters will be at EUSTON POST at 2 p.m. Guides for "D" Company 4th Glosters will be at EUSTON POST at 2.15p.m.

O.C. "B" Company will detail Guides for CHATEAU and CHURCH POSTS to meet "C" Company 4th. Glosters at 2p.m. and "D" Company 4th. Glosters at 2.15p.m.

4. CODE. Code on Completion " JOHNNY WALKER" to the present Battalion Headquarters.

5. STORES. All Stores, Ammunition, Bombs, Tools etc., to be checked as soon as possible ready for handing over. One Officer and one N.C.O. per Company of the 4th. Glosters will be in the trenches to take over about 11a.m. List of Stores to be handed over to be at Battalion Orderly Room at 12 noon on forms supplied. Lists signed by both Officers to be at Battalion Orderly Room by 4p.m.

6. TRANSPORT. The Transport Officer will arrange to have two Limbers for Lewis Guns, Signalling and Sniping Equipment, at The SHRINE at 12 noon. Officers Trench Kits and Mess Boxes to be at The SHRINE by 3p.m. Transport Officer to arrange carriage of same.

7. ROUTE. Companies will march to Billets via the SHRINE - CROIX BARBEE.

8. GUIDES. Billeting Officer will arrange to have Guides to meet incoming Companies to guide them to their Billets. Officers Commanding Companies will report arrival in Billets to Battalion Headquarters.

9. RUE DU PUITS. RUE DU PUITS POST: O.C. "B" Company will arrange for one N.C.O. and 3 men to relieve "D" Company 4th. Glosters at the RUE DU PUITS POST by 1 p.m. This N.C.O. will send the List of the Stores taken over to the Battalion Headquarters as soon as possible after relief.

(Signed) P.H.Beck. Capt.
A/Adjutant. 2/6th. Bn. Gloster Regiment.

Appendix 6.

VERY SECRET.

Operation Order No. 12. by Lt. Col. F.A. LEAH
Commanding 2/6th. Bn. The Gloucestershire Regiment.

Ref: Bethune (Combined)
and Bde. Trench Map.

In The Field.
25. 9. 1916.

1. RELIEF. The 6th. Glosters will relieve 4th. Glosters in POSTS and KEEPS and in Front Line to-morrow 26th. inst. Relief to be Complete by 4p.m.

2. BILLETS. 2nd. Lieut. A. Bickley and 1 N.C.O. per Company will remain behind to hand over Billets. This Officer and the N.C.O's will report to the Adjutant at 9.30a.m. Officers Commanding Companies will see that the Billets are left scrupulously clean, and for this purpose Companies should leave their Billets half an hour before the Company marchesoff.

3. ORDER OF RELIEF.

"C" Company 6th. Glosters will relieve "D" Company 4th. Glosters "Right Company"
"B" Company 6th. Glosters will relieve "C" Company 4th. Glosters "Left Company"
"D" Company 6th. Glosters will relieve "B" Company 4th. Glosters on the left of "B" Line and will Garrison CHATEAU POST.
"A" Company 6th. Glosters will relieve "A" Company 4th. Glosters on the right of "B" Line and will Garrison CHURCH POST.

4. GUIDES. Guides for Snipers, Signallers, and Lewis Gunners will be at EUSTON POST at 11a.m. Guides for "C" Company 6th. Glosters will be at EUSTON POST at 1.30p.m. Guides for "B" Company 6th. Glosters will be at EUSTON POST at 1.45p.m. GUIDES for "D" Company 6th. Glosters will be at EUSTON POST at 2p.m. Guides for "A" Company 6th. Glosters will be at EUSTON POST at 2.15p.m. Headquarters will leave Billets for CURZON POST at 2p.m.

5. ROUTE. CROIX BARBEE - SHRINE - BALUCHI.

6. CODE ON COMPLETION. "BUCKETS PLEASE". to new Battalion Headquarters.

7. BLANKETS. These will be rolled in bundles of 10 securely tied labelled by 9a.m., and the Transport Officer will arrange carriage.

8. TRANSPORT. The Transport Officer will arrange Transport as under:-

(a) Limber for Signallers and Snipers Equipment at 9.15a.m. at Headquarters.

(b) One Limber per Company will report at the various Headquarters at 1p.m.

(c) Transport for Headquarters to be at Battalion Headquarters at 2p.m.

(d) Transport for Officers surplus Kits; The latter must be clearly labelled and be at Battalion Headquarters by 12 noon. Transport Officer will arrange to collect these at 12 noon.

(e) Transport for Blankets to be at Battalion and Company Headquarters by 9a.m.

NOTE:- Transports for Front Line may go as far as GREEN BARN, but must halt under cover.

9 ORDER OF MARCH. Companies will move by Platoons at 100 yards distance as far as CROIX BARBEE, and after that by Sections at 100 yards distance.

10. RUE DU PUIT POST. This Post will be relieved by 4th. Glosters during the morning and Officer Commanding "B" Company will arrange for the Garrison to join his Company.

Contd.

11. RETURNS. (a) O.C. Companies, Lewis Gunners, and Bombers, will render a Disposition Return by 8p.m. 26. 9. 1916.

(b) Defence Scheme to be submitted 24 hours after relief.

(c) List of Stores taken over, by 6p.m. 26. 9. 1916.

(d) Tactical Progress, Ammunition Indents, R.E. Indents to be rendered by 6.30a.m.

(e) Situation Reports to be rendered at 2.45a.m. and 2.45p.m. daily.

(f) Casualty returns to be rendered noon daily.

(Signed) P.H. BECK. Capt.

A/Adjutant. 2/6th. Bn. Gloucestershire Regiment.

Vol 6

Confidential

War Diary

of

2/6th Battalion The Gloucestershire Regiment

from 1. 10. 1916 to 31. 10. 1916

Volume 2.

Page 1

Army Form C. 2118.

Instructions regarding War Diaries and Intelligence Summaries are contained in F. S. Regs., Part II. and the Staff Manual respectively. Title pages will be prepared in manuscript.

WAR DIARY
or
~~INTELLIGENCE SUMMARY~~.
(Erase heading not required.)

2/6 Bn. GLOUCESTERSHIRE REGT.

Place	Date	Hour	Summary of Events and Information	Remarks and references to Appendices
NEUVE CHAPELLE SECTOR	1916 Oct 1		Trenches. quiet.	PHB
do	2		Relief by 7th GLOSTERS. Billets & BOUT DEVILLE	App I PHB
BOUT DEVILLE	3		~~Training~~ Cleaning up & interior economy	PHB
	4		Baths & training	PHB
	5		Training	PHB
	6		do & working parties.	PHB
	7		do do	PHB
	8		~~do~~ Relief of 7th GLOSTERS	App 2 PHB
NEUVE CHAPELLE SECTOR	9		Trenches v. quiet. F.G.C.M. on 4348 Pte MAYS	PHB
	10		do Extended to right to include OXFORD ST. & HILLS POST.	App 3 PHB
	11		Small raid attempted by 2/Lieut HENSON & 25 O.R. with bangalore to help raid by 7th Worcesters on right. 7th WORCESTER Raid failed & our party's bangalore refused to work. Moonlight nearly as light as day. Rescue work by party of "C" Coy. under 2/Lieut CRAMPTON & C.S.M. GREENING helped to bring in 2/7 WORCESTER wounded.	PHB PHB

T2134. Wt. W708–776. 500000. 4/15. Sir J. C. & S.

Instructions regarding War Diaries and Intelligence Summaries are contained in F. S. Regs., Part II. and the Staff Manual respectively. Title pages will be prepared in manuscript.

Army Form C. 2118.

Page 2.

WAR DIARY
or
~~INTELLIGENCE SUMMARY~~.
2/6 Bn. GLOUCESTERSHIRE REGT.

(Erase heading not required.)

Place	Date	Hour	Summary of Events and Information	Remarks and references to Appendices
	1916			
NEUVE CHAPELLE SECTOR	Oct 12		Trenches v. quiet	PHB
	13		do	PHB
	14		Relief by 2/4 GLOSTERS. & move to billets at BOUT DEVILLE	App 3A. PHB
BOUT DEVILLE	15		Interior Economy & medical inspection & working parties.	PHB
	16		Baths & training. Draft of 62 O.R. received.	PHB
	17		Training	PHB
	18		Training.	PHB
	19		do Inspection by B.G.C.	PHB
	20		Relief of 2/4 GLOSTERS in NEUVE CHAPELLE Sector	App 4 PHB
SECTOR NEUVE CHAPELLE	21		Trenches. quiet	PHB
	22		do do	PHB
	23		do do	PHB
	24		do do Draft of 17 O.R. arrived.	PHB
BOUT DEVILLE	25		Relief by 2/4 Glosters. RUE DU PUITS Post taken over.	App 5 PHB
	26		Baths & equipment in billets	PHB
BUSNES	27		Move to BUSNES	App 6 PHB

T2134. Wt. W708–776. 500000. 4/15. Sir J. C. & S.

Instructions regarding War Diaries and Intelligence Summaries are contained in F. S. Regs., Part II. and the Staff Manual respectively. Title pages will be prepared in manuscript.

WAR DIARY
or
~~INTELLIGENCE SUMMARY.~~
(*Erase heading not required.*)

Page 3.
2/6 Bn. GLOUCESTERSHIRE REGT.

Army Form C. 2118.

Place	Date	Hour	Summary of Events and Information	Remarks and references to Appendices
	1916			
BUSNES	Oct 28		Training. (Army Reserve)	MB
"	29		do do	MB
"	30		do do	MB
"	31		do Preparations re move	MB

31/10/16.

P H Beck
Capt & Adj
for Lt Col.
Commdg 2/6 Bn. Glosters Regt.

T2134. Wt. W708—776. 500000. 4/15. Sir J. C. & S.

VERY SECRET.

appendix I

Operation Order No. 13 by Lieut. Colonel F.A.Leah,
Commanding 2/6th Battalion Gloucestershire Regt.,

In the Field.
1.10.16.

1. RELIEF. The 4th Glosters will relieve the 6th Glosters in the Left Sub-section on October 2nd 1916. Relief to be complete by 4 p.m.
6th Glosters will take over billets vacated by the 4th Glosters at BOUT DE VILLE, and also RUE DU PUITS POST.
"A" Company 6th Glosters will be relieved by "C" Company 4th Glosters.
"B" Company 6th Glosters will be relieved by "B" Company 4th Glosters.
"C" Company 6th Glosters will be relieved by "A" Company 4th Glosters.
"D" Company 6th Glosters will be relieved by "D" Company 4th Glosters.

2. BILLETS. 2nd Lieut. S.T.Baron, 1 N.C.O. per Company, and 1 N.C.O Headquarters, will report at Battalion Headquarters at 9 a.m. to proceed to BOUT DE VILLE for the purpose of taking over billets.

3. GUIDES. Guides for Snipers, Lewis Gunners, and Signallers, will be on the LA BASSEE Road at EUSTON POST at 11 am.
Guides for "A" Company 4th Glosters will be at EUSTON POST at 1.30 p.m.
Guides for "B" Company 4th Glosters will be at EUSTON POST at 1.45 p.m.
Guides for "C" Company 4th Glosters will be at EUSTON POST at 2 p.m.
Guides for "D" Company 4th Glosters will be at EUSTON POST at 2.15 p.m.

4. CODE. Code on completion:- "DUCKBOARDS", to be sent to present Battalion Headquarters.

5. STORES. All Stores, Ammunition, Bombs, Tools etc., to be checked as soon as possible ready for handing over. 1 Officer, and 1 N.C.O. per Company of the 4th Glosters will be in the trenches to take over about 11 a.m. Lists of Stores to be handed over to be at Battalion Orderly Room by 12 noon on the forms supplied. Lists of Stores signed by both Officers to be at Battalion Orderly Room by 4 p.m.

6. TRANSPORT. Transport Officer will arrange to have [illegible] limbers for Lewis Guns, Signalling, and Sniping equipment, at GREEN BARN at 12 noon. 1 limber per Company will be at GREEN BARN by 3 p.m. Officers' trench kits, and mess boxes, to be at GREEN BARN by 3 p.m. Transport Officer to arrange carriage of same. The Transport Officer will see that not more than 1 limber is at GREEN BARN at a time.

7. ROUTE. Companies will march to billets via the SHRINE - CROIX BARBEE.

8. GUIDES. Billeting Officer will arrange to have guides to meet incoming Companies to guide them to their billets. Officers Commanding Companies will report arrival in billets to Battalion Headquarters.

9. RUE DU PUITS. RUE DU PUITS POST. O.C. "D" Company will arrange for 1 N.C.O. and 3 men to relieve 4th Glosters at the RUE DU PUITS POST by 1 p.m. O.C. "D" Company will send list of stores taken over to Battalion Headquarters as soon as possible after relief.

(Signed) P.H.BECK Captain.
A/Adjutant, 2/6th Glosters.

VERY SECRET. Appendix 2.

WD

2/6th Battalion The Gloucestershire Regiment.

Operation Orders No. 14 by Lieut. Col. F.A.Leah, Commanding. 7.10.16.

Ref. BETHUNE Combined & Brigade Trench Map.

1. RELIEF. The 6th Glosters will relieve the 4th Glosters in Posts and Keeps in front line to-morrow, October 8th 1916. Relief to be complete by 4 p.m.

2. STORES. 1 Officer and 1 N.C.O. per Company to report at Headqrs. of the 4th Glosters at 10.30 a.m. to-morrow, to take over Stores.

3. BILLETS. 2nd Lieut. S.T.Baron and 1 N.C.O. per Company will remain behind to hand over billets. This Officer and the N.C.Os. will report to the Adjutant at 9.30 a.m.

Officers Commanding Companies will see that the billets are left scrupulously clean, and for this purpose Companies should leave their billets half-an-hour before the Company marches off.

4. ORDER OF RELIEF. "A" Coy. 6th Glosters will relieve "D" Coy. 4th Glosters (Right Company).

"D" Coy. 6th Glosters will relieve "C" Company 4th Glosters, (Left Company).

"B" Company 6th Glosters will relieve "B" Company 4th Glosters on the left of "B" Line, and will garrison CHATEAU POST.

"C" Company 6th Glosters will relieve "A" Company 4th Glosters on the Right of "B" Line, and will garrison CHURCH POST.

5. GUIDES. Guides for Snipers, Signallers, and Lewis Gunners, will be at EUSTON POST at 11 a.m.

Guides for "A" Company 6th Glosters will be at EUSTON POST 1.30 p.m.
Guides for "B" " " " " " " " 2 p.m.
" " "C" " " " " " " " 2.15 p.m.
" " "D" " " " " " " " 1.45 p.m.

Headquarters will leave billets for CURZON POST at 2 p.m.

6. ROUTE. CROIX BARBEE - SHRINE - BALUCHI.

7. CODE ON COMPLETION. "SHOVELS", to new Battalion Headquarters.

8. BLANKETS. These will be rolled in bundles of ten securely tied, and labelled, by ~~6~~ 8 a.m., and Transport Officer will arrange carriage.

9. TRANSPORT. Transport Officer will arrange Transport as under:-

(a) Limber for Signallers, and Snipers equipment at 9.15 a.m. at Battalion Headquarters.
(b) 1 Limber per Company will report at the various Coy. Headqrs. at 12 noon.
(c) Transport for Headquarters to be at Battn. Headqrs. at 2 p.m.
(d) Surplus kits belonging to Officers of "A", "B", and "C" Companies must be clearly labelled and sent to Battalion Headquarters by 12 noon. Transport Officer will arrange to collect these.

Transport Officer will arrange to collect Officers' surplus kits at "D" Company's Headqrs.

(e) Transport for Blankets to be at Battn. and Company Headquarters by ~~9 a.m.~~ 8am.

NOTE: Transport for Front Line may go as far as GREEN BARN, but must halt under cover.

P.T.O.

10. ORDER OF MARCH. Companies will move by Platoons at 100 yards distance as far as CROIX BARBEE, and after that by Sections at 100 yards distance. Strict attention must be paid to March Discipline.

11. RUE DU PUITS POST. This POST will be relieved by the 2/4th Glosters during the morning, and Officer Commanding "D" Company will arrange for the garrison to join his Company

12. RETURNS.
(a) Os. C. Companies, Lewis Gunners, and Bombers, will render a Disposition Return by 8 p.m. 8.10.16.
(b) Defence Scheme to be submitted 24 hours after relief.
(c) List of Stores taken over to reach Battn. Headqrs. by 6 p.m. 8.10.16.
(d) Tactical Progress Reports, Ammunition Indents, R.E. Indents, to be rendered to Battn. Headqrs. by 6.30 a.m. daily.
(e) Situation Reports to reach Battalion Headquarters at 2.45 a.m. and 2.45 p.m. daily.
(f) Casualty Returns to reach Battn. Headqrs. at 12 noon daily.

(Signed) P.H.BECK Captain.
A/Adjutant, 2/5th Glosters.

Appendix 3

Operation Order No. 15 by Lieut. Col. F.A. Leah Commdg.

2/6th Battalion The Gloucestershire Regiment.

Ref: Brigade Trench Map.

In the Field.
9.10.1916.

1. INFORMATION. The 6th Glosters will extend to their Right, and take over the line of the 7th Worcesters up to OXFORD STREET inclusive (i.e. point S.5.c.4.3.).
The 6th Glosters will also take over HILL'S REDOUBT from 7th Worcesters, and EUSTON POST from 8th Worcesters. All moves to be completed by 8 a.m. 10th inst.,

2. RELIEF. (2) "C" Company will take over from Left Company 7th Worcesters, and also HILL'S REDOUBT (Strength 1 platoon: 1 Lewis Gun and Team from "B" Line). The platoon of "C" Company at CHURCH REDOUBT will be relieved by 1 N.C.O. and 6 men of "A" Company. Guides for "C" Company will be at Junction of "B" Line and EDGWARE ROAD at 7 a.m. 10th inst.,

3. POSTS. The O.C. "B" Company will arrange for 1 platoon (Strength 1 N.C.O. and 20 Other Ranks) to take over EUSTON POST from 8th Worcesters. Reliefto be complete by 7.30 a.m.

4. HANDING OVER CERTIFICATES. The usual handing over, and taking over certificates to be handed to Battalion Orderly Room as soon as possible.

5. CODE ON COMPLETION. Code on completion for "C" Company : "PUSH A BIT MORE".

6. RATIONS. Rations for "C" Company will be taken to the St. VAAST Dump, and bought up on trolley to Junction of HUN STREET and "B" Line, after the night of 9.10.1916.

(Signed) P.H.BECK Captain.
Adjutant, 6 Glosters.

ADDENDUM.

Distribution Maps to be rendered to Battalion Orderly Room as soon as possible.

———

Appendix 3A

VERY SECRET.

Operation Order No. 15 dated 13. 10. 1916 by ~~Lt.-Col.~~ Major A.D.Bartleet Commanding 2/6th. Bn. Gloster Regt.

1. RELIEF. The 4th. Glosters will relieve the 6th. Glosters in the Left Sub-Section on October 14th. 1916. Relief to be complete by 4p.m.

6th. Glosters will take over Billets vacated by the 4th. Glosters at BOUT DE VILLE, and also RUE DU PUITS POST.

"A" Coy. 6th Glosters will be relieved by "B" Coy. 4th. Glosters.
"B" " " " " " " "C" " " "
"C" " " " " " " "D" " " "
"D" " " " " " " "A" " " "

The 4th. Gloster Reserve Company will take over POSTS held by 6th. Glosters as under:-

CHATEAU POST - Half Platoon. CHURCH POST - Half Platoon.
HILLS REDOUBT - One Platoon. EUSTON POST - One Platoon.

2. BILLETS. 2nd. Lieut. S.T.Baron. 1 N.C.O. Per Company and 1 N.C.O. for Headquarters will report at Battalion Headquarters at 9a.m. to-morrow to proceed to BOUT DE VILLE for the purpose of taking over Billets.

3. GUIDES. Guides for Snipers, Lewis Gunners, and Signallers, will be on the LA BASSEE Road at EUSTON POST at 11a.m.
Guides for "A" Company 4th. Glosters will be at EUSTON POST at 1.30p.m.
Guides for "B" Company 4th. Glosters will be at EUSTON POST at 1.45p.m.
Guides for "C" Company 4th. Glosters will be at EUSTON POST at 2p.m.
Guides for "D" Company/4th. Glosters will be at EUSTON POST at 2.15p.m., also Guides detailed by O.C. Companies for CHURCH POST, CHATEAU POST, and HILLS REDOUBT.

All Guides must have a written slip showing what they are for.

4. CODE. Code on completion:- "RUM", to be sent to present Battalion Headquarters.

5. STORES. All Stores, Ammunition, Bombs, Tools etc., to be checked as soon as possible, ready for handing over.
1 Officer, and 1 N.C.O. per Company of the 4th. Glosters will be in the Trenches to take over about 11a.m. Lists of Stores to be handed over to be at Battalion Orderly Room by 12 noon on the forms supplied. Lists of Stores signed by both Officers to be at Battalion Orderly Room by 2.30p.m.

6. TRANSPORT. Transport Officer will arrange to have Limbers for Lewis Guns, Signalling, and Sniping Equipment, at the SHRINE at 12 noon. 1 Limber per Company will be at the SHRINE by 3p.m.

Officers Trench Kits, and Mess Boxes, to be at the SHRINE by 3p.m. Transport Officer to arrange carriage for same.

7. ROUTE. Companies will march to Billets via the SHRINE - CROIX BARBEE.

8. GUIDES. Billeting Officer will arrange to have Guides to meet incoming Companies to guide them to their Billets. Officers Commanding Companies will report arrival in Billets to Battalion Headquarters.

9. RUE DU PUITS. RUE DU PUITS POST. O.C. "A" Company will arrange for 1 N.C.O. and 3 men to relieve 4th. Glosters at the RUE DU PUITS POST by 1p.m. "O.C. "A" Company" will send List of Stores taken over to Battalion Headquarters as soon as possible after relief.

(Signed) P.H.BECK. Captain.

A/Adjutant. 2/6th. Bn. Gloster Regiment.

VERY SECRET. *Appendix 4.*

2/6th. Battalion The Gloucestershire Regiment.

Operation Order No. 16 dated 19. 10. 1916. by Major A.D.Bartleet Commanding.

In The Field. 19. 10. 1916.

1. RELIEF. The 6th. Gloucesters will relieve the 4th. Glosters in Posts and Keeps in Front Line to-morrow, October 20th. 1916. Relief to be complete by 4p.m.

2. STORES. One Officer and one N.C.O. per Company to report at the Headquarters of 4th. Glosters at 10.30a.m. to-morrow, to take over Stores.

3. BILLETS. 2nd. Lieut. S.T.BARON and one N.C.O. per Company will remain behind to hand over Billets. This Officer and the N.C.O's will report to the Adjutant at 9.30a.m.
Officers Commanding Companies will see that the Billets are left scrupulously clean, and for this purpose Companies should leave their Billets half an hour before the Company marches off.

4. ORDER OF RELIEF.

"A" Company 6th. Glosters will relieve "C" Company 4th. Glosters in B Line - CHATEAU POST (Half Platoon) - EUSTON POST (One Platoon).

"B" Company 6th. Glosters will relieve "B" Company 4th. Glosters (Centre Company) - CHURCH POST (Half Platoon).

"C" Company 6th. Glosters will relieve "D" Company 4th. Glosters (Right Company) - HILLS POST (One Platoon).

"D" Company 6th. Glosters will relieve "A" Company 4th. Glosters (Left Company) and HUSH HALL.

5. GUIDES. Guides for Snipers, Signallers, and Lewis Gunners, will be at EUSTON POST at 11a.m.
Guides for "A" Company 6th. Glosters will be at EUSTON POST AT 1.30pm.
" " "B" " " " " " " " " " 2p.m.
" " "C" " " " " " " " " " 2.15pm.
" " "D" " " " " " " " " " 1.45pm.
Headquarters will leave Billets for CURZON POST at 2p.m.

6. ROUTE. CROIX BARBEE - SHRINE - BALUCHI.

7. CODE ON COMPLETION. "QUI VIVE" to new Battalion Headquarters.

8. BLANKETS. These will be rolled in bundles of 10 securely tied and labelled, by 8a.m., and the Transport Officer will arrange carraige.

9. TRANSPORT. Transport Officer will arrange Transport as under:-

(a) Limber for Signallers and Snipers Equipment at 9.15a.m. at Battalion Headquarters.
(b) One Limber per Company will report at the various Company Headquarters at ~~2p.m.~~ *Noon*.
(c) Transport for Headquarters to be at Battalion Headquarters at 2p.m.
(d) Surplus Kits belonging to Officers of "A", "B" and "C" Companies must be clearly labelled and sent to Battalion Headquarters by 12 noon. Transport Officer will arrange to collect these.
Transport Officer will arrange to collect Officers surplus Kits at "D" Company Headquarters.
(e) Transport for Blankets to be at Battalion Headquarters and Company Headquarters by 8a.m.
NOTE:- Transport for FRONT LINE may go as far as

SHRINE

as/ ~~GREEN BARN, but must halt under cover.~~

10. ORDER OF MARCH. Companies will move by Platoons at 100 yards distance as far as CROIX BARBEE, and after that by Sections at 100 yards distance. Strict attention must be paid to march discipline.

11. RUE DU PUITS POST. This POST will be relieved by the 4th. Glosters during the morning, and Officer Commanding "A" Company will arrange for the Garrison to join his Company.

12. RETURNS.

(a) Officers Commanding Companies, Lewis Gunners, and Bombers, will render a Disposition Return to Battalion Headquarters by 8p.m. 20. 10. 1916.

(b) Defence Scheme to be submitted 24 hours after relief.

(c) List of Stores taken over to reach Battalion Headquarters by 6p.m. 20. 10. 1916.

(d) Tactical Progress Reports, Ammunition Indents, R.E. Indents, to be rendered to Battalion Headquarters by 6.30a.m. daily.

(e) Situation Reports to reach Battalion Headquarters at 2.45a.m., and 2.45p.m. daily.

(f) Casualty Returns to reach Battalion Headquarters at 12 noon daily.

(Signed). P.H. BECK. Captain.

Adjutant. 2/6th. Battn. Gloucester Regiment.

Appendix 5

VERY SECRET.

Operation Order No. 17 dated 24. 10. 1916 by
Lt. Col. F.A.LEAH Commanding 2/5th. Battn. Gloster Regt.

IN THE FIELD. 24. 10. 1916.

1. RELIEF. The 4th. Glosters will relieve the 6th. Glosters in the Left Sub - Section to-morrow, 25. 10. 1916 Relief to be complete by 4p.m.

6th. Glosters will take over Billets vacated by the 4th. Glosters at BOUT DE VILLE, and also RUE DU PUITS POST.

"A"	Company	6th.	Glosters	will	be	relieved	by	"B"	Company	4th.	Glosters
"B"	"	"	"	"	"	"	"	"D"	"	"	"
"C"	"	"	"	"	"	"	"	"C"	"	"	"
"D"	"	"	"	"	"	"	"	"A"	"	"	"

The 4th. Glosters will take over POSTS held by 6th. Glosters as under:-

CHATEAU POST	- Half Platoon.	CHURCH POST	- Half Platoon.
HILLS.	- One Platoon.	EUSTON.	- One Platoon.

2. BILLETS. 2nd. Lieut. S.T.BARON, One N.C.O. for Company. and 1 N.C.O. for Headquarters will report at Battalion Headquarters at 9a.m. to-morrow to proceed to BOUT DE VILLE for the purpose of taking over Billets.

3. GUIDES. No Guides will berequired.

4 CODE. Code on Completion:- "VERB. SAP." to be sent to present Battalion Headquarters.

5. STORES. All Stores, Ammunition, Bombs, Tools etc., to be checked as soon as possible, ready for handing over.
One Officer, and one N.C.O. per Company of the 4th. Glosters will be in the trenches to take over about 11a.m. List of Stores to be handed over to be at Battalion Orderly Room as early as possible to-morrow morning on the forms supplied. Lists of Stores signed by both Officers to be at Battalion Orderly Room by 2.30p.m.

6. TRANSPORT. Transport Officer will arrange to have limbers for Lewis Guns, Signalling, and Bulping Equipment, at the SHRINE at 12 noon. One Limber per Company will be at the SHRINE by 3p.m.

Officers' Trench Kits, and Mess Boxes, to be at the SHRINE by 5p.m. Transport Officer to arrange carriage for same.

7. ROUTE. Companies will march to Billets via SHRINE - CROIX BARBEE.

8. GUIDES. Billeting Officer will arrange to have Guides to meet Incoming Companies to guide them to their Billets.
Officers Commanding Companies will report arrival in Billets to Battalion Headquarters.

9. RUE DU PUITS. RUE DU PUITS POST. O.C. "B" Company will arrange for one N.C.O. and three men to relieve the 4th. Glosters at the RUE DU PUITS POST by 1p.m.
O.C. "B" Company will send the List of Stores ~~handed~~ taken over to Battalion Headquarters as soon as possible after relief.

(Signed) P.H.BECK. Captain.
Adjutant. 2/5th. Battn. Gloucestershire Regiment.

Appendix 4.

OPERATION ORDER NO. 18 by

LIEUT. COL. F.A.LEAH, O.C. 2/6th Bn. Gloucestershire Regiment.

Ref: Sheet 36a. 1/40,000.

In the Field. 26.10.1916.

Sick Parade 6.30 a.m. Orderly Officer : 2/Lt.P.J.Borrie.

1. INFORMATION. The 2/6th Glosters will be relieved to-morrow 27th inst., by the Queen Victoria Rifles, and be withdrawn into Corps Reserve, occupying billets at BUSNES P.26.

2. STARTING POINT AND ROUTE. The Starting Point will be the Road Junction at R.25.d.2.8. The Route will be FOSSE - Cross Roads R.20.c. - LE CORNET - MALO - Cross Roads Q.26.c. - P.29.b.7.3. - P.29.a.7.0.

3. ORDER OF MARCH. The Battalion will march as per margin. The Head of the Column will pass the Starting point at 9.30a.m. Until reaching Cross Roads W. of FOSSE, Companies will march independently at 200 yards distance. On reaching a point W. of the F in FOSSE Companies will close up and march as a Battalion.

Signallers.
"A" Company.
"B" Company.
"C" Company.
"D" Company.
Battn. Hqrs.

4. POSITION IN COLUMN OF ROUTE. Lewis Gun Carts will be in rear of the Battalion and not with Companies.

5. TRANSPORT. All Transport less Cookers, Maltese Cart, Officers Mess Cart and Water Carts, will precede the Battalion by one hour.

6. MARCH DISCIPLINE. The strictest attention must be paid to March Discipline.

(a) Cooks to be behind and not at the side of Cookers.

(b) The rate of marching must be slow, usual clock hour halts will be observed and opportunity taken to collect stragglers. Troops will invariably march on the right of the road. This also applies to the supernumerary ranks. Platoon Commanders will see that packs are immediately removed, and that files are changed over at the halts. Company Commanders will see that their men have their meals in sufficient time before the march.

(c) Packs of the Transport Serjeant, and of the regimental drivers of 1st. Line Transport vehicles, may be carried on the vehicles. Those of drivers of spare horses and of pack animals will be on the man.

(d) The Leather Jerkin will be worn strapped on the top of the Pack underneath the flap. The ground sheet on the top of the Pack outside flap.

(e) Pioneers will march with their Companies and at long halts, will be responsible for digging Latrines.

(f) All Faeces must be covered with earth by means of the Entrenching Tool.

7. RETURNS. Company Commanders will, immediately on arrival in Billets, render a Falling Out States: this will shew "Distance covered before falling out". No man is allowed to fall out without a written Pass to be shewn to the Second in Command and Medical Officer.

8. BAGGAGE. All Officers Kits, Mess Boxes, Signalling Equipment etc., to be at Battalion Headquarters at 7a.m. Blankets securely and neatly rolled in bundles of ten, and also labelled, to be at Battalion Headquarters at 6.30a.m.

P. T. O.

9. <u>BILLETS.</u> The Orderly Officer, 1 N.C.O. and 4 men per Company will remain behind to hand over and to see that Billets are clean. The Orderly Officer will Obtain receipts in triplicate for Stores etc., handed over, and also obtain a receipt for cleanliness.

This party will march to BUSNES as a party.

10. <u>MEALS.</u> Dinners will be eaten on the way, tea on arrival in Billets. All details will have dinner with their Companies.

(Signed) P.H. BECK. Captain.

Adjutant. 2/6th. Battalion Gloucestershire Regiment.

Confidential

Vol 7

War Diary

of

2/6th Bn: GLOUCESTERSHIRE REGT.

From 1st Nov: 1916 To 30th Nov 1916

Volume 2.

Instructions regarding War Diaries and Intelligence Summaries are contained in F. S. Regs., Part II. and the Staff Manual respectively. Title pages will be prepared in manuscript.

WAR DIARY 2/6 BN. GLOUCESTERSHIRE REGT.

or

~~INTELLIGENCE SUMMARY.~~

(Erase heading not required.)

Army Form C. 2118.

Place	Date	Hour	Summary of Events and Information	Remarks and references to Appendices
	1916			
AUCHEL	NOV 1		March to billets at AUCHEL.	PHB
MONCHY BRETON	2		do MONCHY BRETON.	PHB
FREVILLERS	3		do FREVILLERS	PHB
do	4		Training - best training area since leaving ENGLAND	PHB
TERNAS	5		March to billets at TERNAS	PHB
FORTEL	6		March to billets at FORTEL. Roads on line of march since 1/11/16 on the whole good though maps not a reliable guide for choice of roads. Chief trouble has been lack of boots. On the whole marching has been good. Average weight carried by men from 62-65 lbs.	PHB
do	7		Training & interior economy - light day.	PHB
do	8		Training - especially Lewis Gunners.	PHB
do	9		Training - good country. Baths improvised. Two Coys. bathed.	PHB
do	10		Training.	PHB
do	11		do	PHB
do	12		do	PHB
	13		do	PHB

T2134. Wt. W708—776. 500000. 4/15. Sir J. C. & S.

Instructions regarding War Diaries and Intelligence Summaries are contained in F. S. Regs., Part II. and the Staff Manual respectively. Title pages will be prepared in manuscript.

WAR DIARY
or
~~INTELLIGENCE SUMMARY.~~
(Erase heading not required.)

Army Form C. 2118.

2/6 Bn. GLOUCESTERSHIRE REGT.

Place	Date	Hour	Summary of Events and Information	Remarks and references to Appendices
	1916			
FORTEL ~~[illegible]~~	Nov 14		Training	PHB
BOISBERQUES	15		Move to BOISBERQUES	PHB
St LEGER	16		Move to St LEGER	PHB
AVELUY	17		Move to AVELUY. IInd. Corps. Troops attd 19th DIVISION	PHB
do	18		Huts AVELUY. Reconnaissance of Roads.	PHB
do	19		do. RE work of roads to HAMEL & St PIERRE DIVION	PHB
do	20		do	PHB
do	21		Training. D Coy & 3 platoons B Coy on railway making	PHB
do	22		Preparations for move (orders later cancelled). Railway party as 21st	PHB
do	23		Working Parties.	PHB
do	24		A Coy, D. Coy and 3 platoons B Coy Working Parties. Remainder Training.	A.W.T.
do	25th		Working Parties	A.W.T.
do	26		Working Parties	A.W.T.
do	27		Working Parties	A.W.T.
do	28		Working Parties	A.W.T.
do	29		Working Parties Orders for relief received.	A.W.T.

T2134. Wt. W708—776. 500000. 4/15. Sir J. C. & S.

Instructions regarding War Diaries and Intelligence Summaries are contained in F. S. Regs., Part II. and the Staff Manual respectively. Title pages will be prepared in manuscript.

WAR DIARY 2/6th BN. GLOUCESTERSHIRE REGT.
or
~~INTELLIGENCE SUMMARY~~.
(*Erase heading not required.*)

Army Form C. 2118.

Place	Date	Hour	Summary of Events and Information	Remarks and references to Appendices
AVELUY	1916. Nov 30th		Relief of 2/4th ROYAL BERKS	App. 1 A.W.I.

[illegible] Lt Col
Commanding 2/6th BN. GLOUCESTERSHIRE REGT

T2134. Wt. W708–776. 500000. 4/15. Sir J. C. & S.

Appendix I

SECRET. Operation Orders No. 28 dated 29.11.1916, by Lieut. Col. F.A.Leah, Commanding 2/6th Battalion Gloucestershire Regiment.

Ref: Trench Map 57.D.S.E.

1. **MOVE.**

(a) 183rd Infantry Brigade will relieve the 184th Infantry Brigade on Divisional Front R.17.b.2.7. to R.21.a.8.5. on the night 30/1st December.

(b) 2/6th Glosters less 2 Companies will relieve the 4th Royal Berks in huts at W.10.d. Relief to be complete by 12 noon. Battalion less "A" & "C" Companies will parade on Company parade grounds at 9.45 a.m. ready to move off by 10 a.m.

The Orderly Officer will remain behind to hand over huts to 4th Royal Berks., and will obtain a receipt for stores handed over and a certificate for cleanliness of billets.

2. **BILLETS.**

2nd Lieut. S.T.Baron and 3 N.C.Os. will proceed this afternoon to arrange billets in huts at W.10.d.

3. **WORK COMPANIES.**

"A" & "C" Companies are detailed as Work Companies to relieve 2 Companies of 4th Royal Berks.

"A" Company 6th Glosters will relieve "C" Company 4th R. Berks in FABRIK TRENCH. FABECK

"C" Company 6th Glosters will relieve "A" Company 4th R. Berks as under:

2 Platoons	ZOLLERN REDOUBT.
1 Platoon	THIEPVAL ROAD.
1 "	In shelters SOUTH of MOUQUET FARM.

1 guide per platoon will meet these Companies at GRAVEL PIT R.27.c.4.5. at 1 p.m.

4. **MARCH.**

Intervals of 200 yards will be maintained between "A" & "C" Companies NORTH of line POZIERES - THIEPVAL, troops will proceed at 150 yards between platoons. Relief to be complete by 4 p.m.

5. **ROUTE.**

NAB VALLEY - GRAVEL PIT.

6. **CODE.**

Code for relief complete will be "THELASSA" direct to Brigade H.Q. MOUQUET FARM for "A" & "C" Companies, and also by runner to Battn. H.Q.,

7. **RATIONS.**

Rations for 1st December for "A" & "C" Companies will be carried on the man.

8. **WORKING PARTIES.**

O.C. "D" Company will detail 100 men with a proportion of officers to report at road junction W.16.b.8.8. at 8 a.m. 30.11.16 to Capt. COLLINS 34th Royal Fusileers, and 20 men under an officer to report to Railway Ordnance Officer, station yard at AVELUY at 8 a.m. for loading trains. Haversack rations will be carried. Owing to the fact that units are moving, details for working parties must go to work carrying their full kit, and after work march to new quarters.

P.T.O.

9. <u>BLANKETS</u>.

"B" Company, balance of "D" Company, H.Q. Details etc., will carry their blankets to new billets in huts W.10.d.

Transport Officer will arrange for conveyance of M.Os. Stores, Officers valises, and blankets of "A", "C", and "D" Companies, which will be tied in bundles of ten, and loaded up not later than 9.30a.m. at old Q.M.S. Stores.

Officers' valises, mess boxes, etc., to be ready at the same hour.

O.C. "B" Coy. will detail a loading party of 2 N.C.Os. and 10 men to report to Transport Officer at 9 a.m.

10. <u>DISCIPLINE</u>.

Until further Orders O.C. "A" & "C" Companies will render all reports and returns direct to Brigade.

11. O.C. "B" Company will det N.C.O. and 3 men to report to Brigade Bombing Officer ~~at X.1.d.5.5.~~ to-morrow, and will take over not later than 2 p.m. They will be in charge of Brigade Bomb Store.

Unexpended days rations, and rations for Dec, 1st will be carried. They will afterwards be ration by LEFT BATTALION in the line. Names to be sent into the Orderly Room by 9 p.m. to-night. O.C. "B" Company will also detail 1 L/cpl. and 8 men to report to Brigade Transport Officer at TULLOCK'S CORNER. Work:- pushing and carrying parties for rations, ammunition, and R.E. Stores, between TULLOCK'S CORNER and RIFLE DUMP.

Rations for Dec, 1st to be carried on the man and afterwards they will be rationed by RIGHT FRONT BATTN. (8th Worcesters).

12. <u>CLOTHING</u>.

Companies going up to the line will wear steel helmets and jerkins. Great Coats and ground sheets to be carried.

Blankets, packs, and S.D. Caps will not be taken.

Packs of "A" & "C" Companies will be taken up to forward distributing point at GRAVEL PIT R.27.c.4.5. either by pack mules or mule-drawn tram-route under arrangements made by Transport Officer. Beyond this they will be man-handled.

14. <u>WATER & R.E. STORES</u>.

Water will be conveyed in a similar manner.

R.E. Stores may be obtained from R.E. Dump at GRAVEL PIT WHEN FORMED.

15. <u>WATER</u>.

All ranks are warned as to the necessity of economising both in water and food. The return of petrol tins from all portions of the line to forward distributing centre is absolutely essential.

16. <u>CARE OF FEET</u>.

Os. C. "A" & "C" Companies will at once see that whale oil, if not already drawn, is obtained from Q.M. Stores.

Platoon Commanders are held directly responsible for seeing that the mens' feet are rubbed prior to moving. Each man should take a spare pair of socks with him into the trenches.

17. <u>CLOTHING</u>.

O.C. "A" & "C" Companies must do their best to see that their men are warmly clothed. If any men are short of jerkins or Great Coats they should be obtained from men employed in Q.M. Stores and Transport.

18. <u>RUM</u>.

Rum ration, if available, will primarily be distributed to "A" & "C" Companies.

19. <u>BILLETS</u>.

All ranks must be clear of their present billets not later than 10 a.m. Huts to be left as clean as possible.

(sd) A.W.TRATMAN 2/Lieut.
A/Adjutant, 2/6th Glosters.

Vol 8

CONFIDENTIAL.

WAR DIARY.

2/6 GLOSTERS.

DECEMBER 1916.

Confidential

War Diary

of

4th Battn. The Gloucestershire Regt.

From Decr 1st 1916 To Decr 31st 1916

Volume 2

Instructions regarding War Diaries and Intelligence Summaries are contained in F. S. Regs., Part II. and the Staff Manual respectively. Title pages will be prepared in manuscript.

WAR DIARY ~~or INTELLIGENCE SUMMARY.~~ 2/6th BN: GLOUCESTERSHIRE REGT.

(Erase heading not required.)

Army Form C. 2118.

Place	Date	Hour	Summary of Events and Information	Remarks and references to Appendices
	1916			
AVELUY	Dec: 1		"A"+"C" Coys in support trenches. Working Parties for R.E.s "B"+"D" Coys training	A.W.Y.
do	2		All companies on Working Parties.	A.W.Y.
do	3		All companies on Working Parties. Orders for relief of 2/4th GLOSTERS received	A.W.Y.
do	4		Working parties	A.W.Y.
do	5		Relief of 2/4th GLOSTERS in trenches, 2/7th WORCESTERS on our RIGHT	A.W.Y.
TRENCHES	6		Occupation of DESIRE, REGINA and HESSIAN trenches S. of GRANDCOURT	A.W.Y.
do	7		Quiet. Intermittent bombardment by hostile artillery.	A.W.Y.
do	8		Quiet. 3 prisoners (1 officer, 1 NCO + 1 man) captured in front of DESIRE TRENCH	A.W.Y.
do	9		Intermittent bombardment	A.W.Y.
do	10		Intermitten bombardment during day. Relieved by 2/5th WARWICKS. Artillery active during relief, causing some casualties. Move to billets in MARTINSAART WOOD	A.W.Y.
MARTINSAART WOOD	11		Resting.	A.W.Y.
VARENNES	12		Move to huts at VARENNES	PHB

T2134. Wt. W708—776. 500000. 4/15. Sir J. C. & S.

Instructions regarding War Diaries and Intelligence Summaries are contained in F. S. Regs., Part II. and the Staff Manual respectively. Title pages will be prepared in manuscript.

WAR DIARY or ~~INTELLIGENCE SUMMARY~~. 2/6 BN. GLOUCESTERSHIRE REGT.

(Erase heading not required.)

Army Form C. 2118.

Place	Date	Hour	Summary of Events and Information	Remarks and references to Appendices
1916	1916			
VARENNES	Dec 13		Cleaning up & improving Camp. Interior Economy.	PHB
"	14		Training & improving Camp.	PHB
"	15		do do	PHB
"	16		do do	PHB
"	17		do do	PHB
"	18		do do	PHB
"	19		do do	PHB
"	20		do do	PHB
"	21		do do	PHB
MARTINSART WOOD.	22		Move to huts at MARTINSART WOOD. To relieve 182nd Brigade.	PHB
do	23		Working parties	PHB
do	24		do	PHB
do	25		do	PHB
do	26		do	PHB
do	27		do	PHB

T2134. Wt. W708—776. 500000. 4/15. Sir J. C. & S.

Instructions regarding War Diaries and Intelligence Summaries are contained in F. S. Regs., Part II. and the Staff Manual respectively. Title pages will be prepared in manuscript.

WAR DIARY
or
~~INTELLIGENCE SUMMARY.~~
(Erase heading not required.)

2/6 Bn. GLOUCESTERSHIRE REGT.

Army Form C. 2118.

Place	Date	Hour	Summary of Events and Information	Remarks and references to Appendices
	1916			
TRENCHES NR GRANDCOURT	DEC 28		Relief of 7th OX & BUCKS Lt. Infy. Complete 2 am. – much delayed by left Coy. who captured 2 prisoners. 6th BORDER REGT. on left. 7th WORCESTERS on right.	PHB
do	29		Trenches. Nothing unusual	PHB
do	30		do do	PHB
do	31		do do	PHB

A L Bartlett Major.
Commdg.
2/6 Bn. Gloucestershire Regt.
Jan 2. 1917

T2134. Wt. W708—776. 500000. 4/15. Sir J. C. & S.

Confidential

Vol 9

War Diary

of

2/6th Bn: The Gloucestershire Regt.

From 1. 1. 17 To 31. 1. 17

Volume 3

Instructions regarding War Diaries and Intelligence Summaries are contained in F. S. Regs., Part II. and the Staff Manual respectively. Title pages will be prepared in manuscript.

Army Form C. 2118.

WAR DIARY ~~or INTELLIGENCE SUMMARY.~~ 2/6th BATTN GLOUCESTERSHIRE REGT.

(Erase heading not required.)

Place	Date	Hour	Summary of Events and Information	Remarks and references to Appendices
WARWICK HUTS	1917 Jan 1		Trenches. Relief by 1/4 GLOSTERS complete at 9.55 pm. Move to huts and Dugouts (WARWICK HUTS and Dugouts R32c7.0 & R26b). LIEUT. COL. LEAH proceeded to ENGLAND	PHB
do	2		Huts working parties & cleaning up.	PHB
do	3		do do	PHB
do	4		do do	PHB
do	5		do do	PHB
do	6		Move to Huts in MARTINSART WOOD vacated by 2/5th WARWICKS	PHB
MARTINSART WOOD	7		cleaning up & working parties.	PHB
HEDAUVILLE	8		Move to Billets at HEDAUVILLE	PHB
do	9		cleaning up & interior economy	PHB
do	10		Training	PHB
do	11		Training – Baths	AWJ
do	12		Training	AWJ
do	13		Training	AWJ
do	14		Day of rest – cleaning up.	AWJ

T2134. Wt. W708—776. 500000. 4/15. Sir J. C. & S.

Army Form C. 2118.

Instructions regarding War Diaries and Intelligence Summaries are contained in F. S. Regs., Part II. and the Staff Manual respectively. Title pages will be prepared in manuscript.

WAR DIARY
~~or~~ 2/6th BATTN: GLOUCESTERSHIRE. REGT.
~~INTELLIGENCE SUMMARY.~~
(*Erase heading not required.*)

Place	Date	Hour	Summary of Events and Information	Remarks and references to Appendices
	1917			
HEDAUVILLE	Jan 15th		Training	A.W.T.
do	16		Move to RAINCHEVAL	A.W.T.
RAINCHEVAL	17		Move to BOISBERGUES	A.W.T.
BOISBERGUES	18		Move to PROUVILLE	A.W.T.
PROUVILLE	19		Move to ARGENVILLERS	A.W.T.
ARGENVILLERS	20		Cleaning up and interior economy	A.W.T.
do	21		Day of rest	A.W.T.
do	22		Cleaning up and interior economy	A.W.T.
do	23		Morning – Platoon and Company training – Afternoon – Recreational training	A.W.T.
do	24		do do	A.W.T.
do	25		do do	A.W.T.
do	26		do do	A.W.T.
do	27		do do	A.W.T.
do	28		Day of Rest ~~do~~ Divine Service	A.W.T.
do	29		Morning – Platoon and Company training : Afternoon – Recreational training	A.W.T.
do	30		do do	A.W.T.
do	31		do do	A.W.T.

A D Bartlett Major
Comdg 2/6th Glouster Regt.

T2134. Wt. W708–776. 500000. 4/15. Sir J. C. & S.

Confidential

Vol. 10

War Diary

of

2/6th BATTN: The GLOUCESTERSHIRE REGT:

From 1. 2. 17 To 28. 2. 17.

Volume 3.

W. 10

Instructions regarding War Diaries and Intelligence Summaries are contained in F. S. Regs., Part II. and the Staff Manual respectively. Title pages will be prepared in manuscript.

Army Form C. 2118.

WAR DIARY ~~or~~ ~~INTELLIGENCE SUMMARY.~~ 2/6th BATTN: GLOUCESTERSHIRE. REGT.

(Erase heading not required.)

Place	Date	Hour	Summary of Events and Information	Remarks and references to Appendices
	1917			
ARGENVILLERS	Feb. 1		Morning – Platoon and Company Training: Afternoon – Recreational Training	A.W.T.
do	" 2		do do	A.W.T
do	" 3		Training – Battalion in attack	A.W.T
do	" 4.		MOVE to AILLY-LE-HAUT-CLOCHER	A.W.T
AILLY le haut Clocher	" 5.		Cleaning billets – 2 hours training	A.W.T
do	" 6		Training	A.W.T
do	" 7		Training – Night work	A.W.T
do	" 8		Training – Night work	A.W.T.
do	" 9		Training – Battalion in attack	A.W.T
do	" 10		Training – ditto	A.W.T
do	" 11		Day of rest – Services – Interior Economy – Preparation for move of transport	A.W.T
do	" 12		Training. – Transport moves to ARGOUEVES	A.W.T
do	" 13		Transport moves to AUBIGNY – Preparations for move of personnel	A.W.T.
do	" 14		Transport moves to DEMUIN. Battalion marches to PONT REMY station, and	A.W.T
	" 15		entrains for WIENCOURT. From WEINCOURT the Battalion marches to billets in DEMUIN	

T2134. Wt. W708—776. 500000. 4/15. Sir J. C. & S.

Instructions regarding War Diaries and Intelligence Summaries are contained in F. S. Regs., Part II. and the Staff Manual respectively. Title pages will be prepared in manuscript.

WAR DIARY of 2/6th BATTN: the GLOUCESTERSHIRE REGT.

~~INTELLIGENCE SUMMARY~~

(Erase heading not required.)

Army Form C. 2118.

Place	Date	Hour	Summary of Events and Information	Remarks and references to Appendices
	1917			
DEMUIN	Feb 15th		Rest – Preparation for move	A.W.T.
do	16th		Move to billets in WIENCOURT	A.W.T.
WIENCOURT	17th		Training – {183 Inf: Bde: relieves 1 Battn of 101st French I. Regt in PRESSOIRE sector and 2 Battns 130th French I. Regt in KRATZ Sector}	A.W.T.
do	18th		Move to billets in FRAMERVILLE to form Battalion in Brigade Reserve	A.W.T.
FRAMERVILLE	19th		Specialist Training	A.W.T.
do	20th		Training – Reconnaissance of the Brigade Front	A.W.T.
do	21.		Preparation for trenches – Relief of 2/4th Glosters in the KRATZ SECTION Relief complete by 9 AM 22nd inst. Trenches quiet: muddy	A.W.T.
TRENCHES	22		Day misty – trenches quiet	A.W.T.
do	23		Day misty – trenches quiet. At 7.50 P.M. the enemy heavily bombarded the line of LEFT COY of the Battalion on our RIGHT (2/8th WORCESTERS). Our barrage applied promptly. Apparently a dummy raid. Casualties slight	A.W.T.
do	24		Day clearer – increased artillery activity. Dummy raid carried out by our artillery (combined with coloured lights) on front of LEFT COY of battalion on our RIGHT. Point of entry S 29. d. 4.8.	A.W.T.

T2134. Wt. W708–776. 500000. 4/15. Sir J. C. & S.

Instructions regarding War Diaries and Intelligence Summaries are contained in F. S. Regs., Part II. and the Staff Manual respectively. Title pages will be prepared in manuscript.

WAR DIARY
of 2/6th BATTN: THE GLOUCESTERSHIRE REGT.

~~INTELLIGENCE SUMMARY.~~

(Erase heading not required.)

Army Form C. 2118.

Place	Date	Hour	Summary of Events and Information	Remarks and references to Appendices
	1917			
TRENCHES	Feb 25th		Day very clear – Hostile artillery more active. Relief by the 2/7th ROYAL WARWICKS. Relief completed without incident.	A.W.T.
do	26th		Relief complete 6. AM. Return to billets in FRAMERVILLE	A.W.T.
FRAMERVILLE	27th		Rest and cleaning up. Inspections. Interior economy	A.W.T.
do	28th		Company training. Baths.	A.W.T.

A K Bartlett Major
Comdg 2/6th Battn: the Gloucestershire Regt.

T2134. Wt. W708–776. 500000. 4/15. Sir J. C. & S.

Vol XI

CONFIDENTIAL

WAR DIARY

OF

2/6 BATTN THE GLOUCESTERSHIRE REGT

FROM 1·3·17 TO 31·3·17

(VOLUME 3)

Instructions regarding War Diaries and Intelligence Summaries are contained in F. S. Regs., Part II. and the Staff Manual respectively. Title pages will be prepared in manuscript.

WAR DIARY

~~or~~

~~INTELLIGENCE SUMMARY.~~

(*Erase heading not required.*)

2/6th BN GLOUCESTERSHIRE REGT

Army Form C. 2118.

Place	Date	Hour	Summary of Events and Information	Remarks and references to Appendices
	1917 MARCH			
FRAMERVILLE	1.		Training	AAB
"	2		Training	AAB
"	3		Training	AAB
"	4		Training	AAB
"	5		Training	AAB
"	6		Training	AAB
"	7		General inspections under Company arrangements prior to going into the line	AAB
TRENCHES	8		Relieved 2/5 R WARWICK Regt in Brigade Support at VERMANDOVILLERS. 2 Coys at	AAB
"			VERMANDOVILLERS. 2 Coys at PARISON (Gravel Pits)	AAB
"	9		"A" Coy moved from PARISON to HIBOU Trench - C Coy from PARISON to GUILLAUME Trench.	AAB
"	10		All Companies on working and Carrying parties	AAB
"	11		All Companies on working and Carrying parties	AAB
"	12		Major E.C SLADE 1/4th GLOSTER Regt assumed command. Bde O.O. No 95 received to relieve	AAB
			2/4th GLOSTERS on night 14/15th	AAB
"	13		Arrangements prior to taking over line - C.O forward to see O.C 2/4th GLOSTERS	AAB
"	14		Relieved 2/4 GLOSTERS in the LEFT Sub section. 3 Companies in line. 1 Company in Support.	AAB

T2134. Wt. W708-776. 500000. 4/15. Sir J. C. & S.

Army Form C. 2118.

WAR DIARY

~~or~~

~~INTELLIGENCE SUMMARY.~~ 2/6 GLOUCESTERSHIRE REGT.

(Erase heading not required.)

Instructions regarding War Diaries and Intelligence Summaries are contained in F. S. Regs., Part II. and the Staff Manual respectively. Title pages will be prepared in manuscript.

Place	Date	Hour	Summary of Events and Information	Remarks and references to Appendices
	MARCH			
TRENCHES	15		Relief complete at 4 am. Night very dark + wet. Day quiet	AHB
"	16		Quiet night, very dark. Patrols out at various times. ~~[illegible]~~	AHB
"	[illegible]		Information received from Bde that enemy was evacuating trenches + withdrawing on	AHB
			to high ground – Patrols went out at 5.30 am + brought back information that	AHB
			the enemy was still there, strength approximately one man to every 20 to 25 yards.	AHB
			casualties 2. Fires seen behind enemy lines.	AHB
"	17		Bde O.O. received for a raid. At 11 am information received that the enemy had	AHB
			definitely evacuated front line. Immediately organised strong Fighting patrols	AHB
			who advanced to enemy front line and found them empty. These patrols	AHB
			established strong points at various places in GERMAN Front Line. Small patrols	AHB
			were then sent forward to make reconnaissance. These patrols penetrated as far	AHB
			as GERMAN 3rd line. No enemy were encountered although it was reported that	AHB
			he still held CHAULNES. Night very quiet. More fires observed behind enemy	AHB
			line. These appeared to be some miles away –	AHB
"	18		Advanced. 3 companies in line 1 in support. Occupied Railway line between	AHB
			HYENCOURT le GRAND and B de LANDSHUT with outposts at PERTAIN. No sign of enemy	AHB
			Battalion HQ moved to BRUST COPSE.	

T2134. Wt. W708–776. 500000. 4/15. Sir J. C. & S.

Instructions regarding War Diaries and Intelligence Summaries are contained in F. S. Regs., Part II. and the Staff Manual respectively. Title pages will be prepared in manuscript.

WAR DIARY ~~or INTELLIGENCE~~ SUMMARY.

(*Erase heading not required.*)

2/6 GLOUCESTERSHIRE REGT

Army Form C. 2118.

Place	Date	Hour	Summary of Events and Information	Remarks and references to Appendices
	MARCH			
BRUST COPSE	19		Advanced 2 companies in line 1 Coy in support 1 Coy in Reserve to MORCHAIN. No enemy encountered. All villages had been blown up or burnt and every tree had been cut down & all stores removed. Dispositions in evening 2 Companies MORCHAIN 1 Coy MILL DE MORCHAIN 1 Outpost Coy at BETHANCOURT. Battalion HQ moved to MORCHAIN	
MORCHAIN	20		Found that Bridges crossing SOMME had been blown up and craters blown at all cross roads. Impossible to advance further. Work on making temporary roads round craters & assisting RE	
"	21		Work on roads & craters also making billets	
"	22		1 Coy making strong points along river. 1 Coy working on craters. 1 Coy on craters & billet repairs.	
"	23		1 Coy making strong points along river. 2 Coys working on craters on East of river 1 Coy on craters West of river.	
"	24		All companies on making defensive line at BETHENCOURT	
"	25		Moved to BETHENCOURT. Relieved at MORCHAIN, by 2/7 WORCESTERS.	
BETHENCOURT	26		Work on craters	

T2134. Wt. W708–776. 500000. 4/15. Sir J. C. & S.

Instructions regarding War Diaries and Intelligence Summaries are contained in F. S. Regs., Part II. and the Staff Manual respectively. Title pages will be prepared in manuscript.

WAR DIARY

~~or~~

~~INTELLIGENCE SUMMARY.~~ 2/6th GLOUCESTERSHIRE REGT.

(Erase heading not required.)

Army Form C. 2118.

Place	Date	Hour	Summary of Events and Information	Remarks and references to Appendices
BETHENCOURT	MARCH 27		Work on Craters. C.O. Adj and Coy Commanders made reconnaisance of ground	AHB
			to be occupied EAST of COULAINCOURT.	AHB
"	28		Moved by night to MONCHY LEGACHE into Brigade Reserve.	AHB
MONCHY LEGACHE	29		All Companies working on crater at MONCHY.	AHB
"	30		All companies working on crater TERTRY	AHB
"	31		All companies working on crater MONCHY. A + C Companies moved in evening to	AHB
			TREFCON.	

[signature]
Lt Col
Comdg 2/6 Glostr Regt.

Vol 12

CONFIDENTIAL

WAR DIARY

of

2/6th Battn GLOUCESTERSHIRE Regt

FROM 1-4-17 TO 30-4-17

(VOLUME 3)

Instructions regarding War Diaries and Intelligence Summaries are contained in F. S. Regs., Part II. and the Staff Manual respectively. Title pages will be prepared in manuscript.

WAR DIARY

~~or~~

~~INTELLIGENCE SUMMARY.~~ 2/6th Bn GLOUCESTERSHIRE REGT.

(Erase heading not required.)

Army Form C. 2118.

Place	Date	Hour	Summary of Events and Information	Remarks and references to Appendices
	1917 april			
MONCHY LE CACHE and TREFCON	1		All Coys working on Craters. The Battn moved in evening to VILLEVEQUE and later to ATILLY.	
St QUENTIN WOOD	2		B + D Coys occupied HOLNON and St QUENTIN wood. C Coy in support. A Coy + Battn H.Q at ATILLY. No trace of the enemy were found and posts were established in front of St QUENTIN WOOD. D Coy + Battn H.Q at KEEPERS LODGE St QUENTIN WOOD.	
"	3		In the evening 1 platoon of C Coy moved forward to reconnoitre wood at S 32 A+B (MAP 62B-S.W) after short encounter with enemy outpost, we occupied the wood and established posts. 1 O.R. killed.	
"	4		During the afternoon we sent out a patrol of 1 Officer and 1 O.R to reconnoitre wood in M 26 d- (Map 62 B. S.W). which had been occupied by the enemy on night of 3/4th april. Wood was not occupied + we then established a Lewis Gun Post.	
"	5		Battn attacked FRESNOY LE PETIT (Map ref. 62B-SW M 27 a.b) after dark. A and B Coys made the attack. C Coy in support. D Coy in reserve. Battn H.Q. moved to M 32 b 3.3. Three attempts were made to occupy the village, without artillery preparation, but these attacks failed, owing to M.G. fire and wire entanglements. Casualties 4 killed and 10 wounded.	

T2134. Wt. W708—776. 500000. 4/15. Sir J. C. & S.

Instructions regarding War Diaries and Intelligence Summaries are contained in F. S. Regs., Part II. and the Staff Manual respectively. Title pages will be prepared in manuscript.

WAR DIARY

~~or~~

~~INTELLIGENCE SUMMARY.~~ 2/6 BN GLOUCESTERSHIRE REGT

(*Erase heading not required.*)

Army Form C. 2118.

Place	Date	Hour	Summary of Events and Information	Remarks and references to Appendices
	1917 April			
St Quentin WOOD	6		Battn relieved in early morning by 2/4 GLOS REGT. We then became Battn in support. Reld later by Battn in reserve (2/7th WORCESTER) and marched to TERTRY, taking over billets vacated by 2/7th WARWICK REGT. We then became a Battn of Brigade in Divl Reserve	
TERTRY	7		Day devoted to cleaning and repairing billets	
"	8		Battn worked on crater at POEUILLY	
"	9		" " " " " " and later moved to ENNEMAIN, taking over billets of 17th W. YORKS Regt – 18th H L I took over our billets in TERTRY	
ENNEMAIN	10		All Coys working on roads, in vicinity of ENNEMAIN	
"	11		Two Coys " " " " " " and 2 Coys. TRAINING	
"	12		" " " " " " " " " " " "	
"	13		" " " " " " " " " " " "	
"	14		" " " " " " " " " " " "	
"	15		" " " " " " " " " " " "	
"	16		" " " " " " " " " " " "	
"	17		All Coys working on roads, in vicinity of ENNEMAIN.	
"	18		Two " " " " " " " and 2 Coys TRAINING	

T2134. Wt. W708–776. 500000. 4/15. Sir J. C. & S.

Instructions regarding War Diaries and Intelligence Summaries are contained in F. S. Regs., Part II. and the Staff Manual respectively. Title pages will be prepared in manuscript.

WAR DIARY

~~or~~

~~INTELLIGENCE SUMMARY.~~

(Erase heading not required.)

Army Form C. 2118.

Place	Date	Hour	Summary of Events and Information	Remarks and references to Appendices
	1917 April			
ENNEMAIN	19		Battn training	
"	20		Two Coys working on roads in vicinity of ENNEMAIN and 2 Coys TRAINING	
"	21		all Coys working on roads between DEVISE and TERTRY Later the Battn moved to BEAUVOIS, and relieved 2nd Royal Innis Fus. (32 Div)	
BEAUVOIS	22		Day devoted to cleaning and repairing billets	
"	23		TRAINING and work on billets	
"	24		- do -	
"	25		Work on crater and roads at ETTRELLIERS. Later Battn moved to VAUX (1 Coy. and Battn H.Q.) and ETTRELLIERS (3 Coys)	
VAUX and ETTRELLIERS	26		Work on craters and roads in vicinity of the two villages	
"	27		Baths at GERMAINE and TRAINING	
"	28		all Coys working on roads and craters	
"	29		Battn TRAINING	
"	30		All Coys working on roads and craters.	

[signature]

Lieut Col: Comdg
2/6 Gloster Regt.

T2134. Wt. W708—776. 500000. 4/15. Sir J. C. & S.

CONFIDENTIAL.

Vol 13

1861

WAR DIARY

of the

2/6th BATTALION, THE GLOUCESTERSHIRE REGIMENT.

from 1.5.17 to 30.5.17

(VOLUME 3)

Instructions regarding War Diaries and Intelligence Summaries are contained in F. S. Regs., Part II. and the Staff Manual respectively. Title pages will be prepared in manuscript.

WAR DIARY

or

~~INTELLIGENCE SUMMARY.~~ 2/6th BATTN GLOUCESTERSHIRE REGIMENT

(Erase heading not required.)

Army Form C. 2118.

Place	Date	Hour	Summary of Events and Information	Remarks and references to Appendices
	1917 MAY			
VAUX and ETREILLERS	1		1½ companies working on roads. 2½ companies training. Presentation of Parchments by G.O.C. Brigade during afternoon.	C.H.C.
"	2		Relieved 4th Royal Berkshire Regiment and 1 company of Bucks Battalion in left section of HOLNON sector, without incident, during the evening.	C.H.C.
TRENCHES	3		Quiet day. The ordinary amount of shelling.	C.H.C.
"	4		Quiet day.	C.H.C.
"	5		Quiet day. Intermittent artillery fire.	C.H.C.
"	6		Relief by 2/7th WORCESTER REGIMENT. We become battalion in reserve.	C.H.C.
HOLNON WOOD	7		Working parties by night – wiring.	C.H.C.
"	8		Working parties by day + night, wiring.	C.H.C.
"	9		Working parties by day + night, wiring.	C.H.C.
"	10		Working parties by day. Relieved 2/4th GLOUCESTERSHIRE REGIMENT in the evening, + became Right Battalion in Support.	C.H.C.
"	11		Working parties by day, + night – wiring, + carrying.	C.H.C.
"	12		Working parties by day, + night – wiring.	C.H.C.

T2134. Wt. W708—776. 500000. 4/15. Sir J. C. & S.

Instructions regarding War Diaries and Intelligence Summaries are contained in F. S. Regs., Part II. and the Staff Manual respectively. Title pages will be prepared in manuscript.

WAR DIARY
or
~~INTELLIGENCE SUMMARY~~. 2/6th BATTN GLOUCESTERSHIRE REGIMENT
(Erase heading not required.)

Army Form C. 2118.

Place	Date 1917 MAY	Hour	Summary of Events and Information	Remarks and references to Appendices
HOLNON WOOD	13		Working parties by day, + night – wiring + carrying	C+C
"	14		Working parties by day, + night – wiring.	C+C
"	15		Small working parties by day. Relief by Battalion 139th French Infantry Regiment, at night. Battalion moved back to billets in BEAUVOIS	C+C
BEAUVOIS.	16		Day devoted to cleaning, + rest.	C+C
"	17		Marched from BEAUVOIS to billets in NESLE in early morning, arriving mid-day. Remainder of day a rest.	C+C
NESLE	18		Entrained at NESLE, and travelled to LONGEAU, where the Battalion detrained in the morning and marched to billets in COISY. Arrival at COISY at mid-day.	C+C
COISY	19		All companies and specialists training during the morning	C+C
"	20		All companies and specialists training during the morning	C+C
"	21		Battalion marched from COISY to billets in BEAUVAL	C+C
BEAUVAL	22		All companies for C.O's inspection and training during morning. Specialists training morning + afternoon.	C+C

T2134. Wt. W708—776. 500000. 4/15. Sir J. C. & S.

Army Form C. 2118.

Instructions regarding War Diaries and Intelligence Summaries are contained in F. S. Regs., Part II. and the Staff Manual respectively. Title pages will be prepared in manuscript.

WAR DIARY

or

~~INTELLIGENCE SUMMARY~~. 2/6th BATTN GLOUCESTERSHIRE REGIMENT

(Erase heading not required.)

Place	Date	Hour	Summary of Events and Information	Remarks and references to Appendices
	1917 MAY			
BEAUVAL.	23		Battalion marched from BEAUVAL to GRAND RULLECOURT. arrival in billets during afternoon.	CHC
GRAND RULLECOURT	24		Battalion move to ARRAS. March from GRAND RULLECOURT to LE-BAC-DE-SUD on ARRAS-DOULLENS road – from there in motor lorries to ~~billets~~ barracks in ARRAS.	CHC
ARRAS	25		Day devoted to cleaning and company inspections.	CHC
"	26		All companies training morning and afternoon. small company patrol training by night. One company at baths.	CHC
"	27		All companies training in morning. & afterwards church parade	CHC
"	28		All companies training during morning	CHC
"	29		All companies training during morning	CHC
"	30		All companies training during morning	CHC
"	31		Day devoted to interior economy & inspections.	CHC

C H Slade[?] Lt. Col.
2/6th Glouc. Regt.

T2134. Wt. W708–776. 500000. 4/15. Sir J. C. & S.

CONFIDENTIAL

Vol 14

WAR DIARY

of the

2/6th BATTALION THE GLOUCESTERSHIRE REGIMENT

from 1.6.17 to 30.6.17

(VOLUME 3)

A.14

Instructions regarding War Diaries and Intelligence Summaries are contained in F. S. Regs., Part II. and the Staff Manual respectively. Title pages will be prepared in manuscript.

WAR DIARY

~~or~~

~~INTELLIGENCE SUMMARY~~.

(*Erase heading not required.*) 2/6th BATT^N^ GLOUCESTERSHIRE REGIMENT.

Army Form C. 2118.

Place	Date	Hour	Summary of Events and Information	Remarks and references to Appendices
	1917 JUNE			
ARRAS	1		Day devoted to bathing + cleaning. Moved to TILLOY in evening and relieved 2/5th Batt^n^ GLOUC Reg^t^, by midnight.	
TILLOY	2		All companies training during morning, and night patrols.	
"	3		Day of rest. Improvements to shelters.	
"	4		All companies, and specialists training.	
"	5		All companies and specialists training.	
"	6		All companies and specialists training.	
"	7		All companies and specialists training.	
"	8		All companies and specialists training	
"	9		All companies and specialists training.	
"	10		Day devoted to cleaning and rest. Moved to SIMENCOURT during evening. Arrived 1 AM	
SIMENCOURT.	11		Day devoted to cleaning and rest.	
"	12		All companies and specialists training. Sports practice	
"	13		All companies and specialists training. Sports practice	
"	14		All companies and specialists training Sports practice	

Instructions regarding War Diaries and Intelligence Summaries are contained in F. S. Regs., Part II. and the Staff Manual respectively. Title pages will be prepared in manuscript.

WAR DIARY

~~or~~

~~INTELLIGENCE SUMMARY~~.

(*Erase heading not required.*) 2/6 Battn Gloucestershire Regiment

Army Form C. 2118.

Place	Date	Hour	Summary of Events and Information	Remarks and references to Appendices
	1917 JUNE			
SIMENCOURT	15		All companies and specialists training. Sports practice.	
"	16		All companies and specialists training. Sports practice.	
"	17		Day of rest. Brigade sports.	
"	18		All companies and specialists training.	
"	19		All companies and specialists training.	
"	20		Day of rest. Brigade sports.	
"	21		Day devoted to cleaning and inspections.	
"	22		Moved to OEUF. Marched to GOUY-EN-ARTOIS where Battalion entrained. Detrained at HESDIN, and marched to OEUF.	
OEUF.	23		Day devoted to rest and cleaning.	
"	24		Church parade and rest.	
"	25		All companies and specialists training.	
"	26		All companies and specialists training.	
"	27		All companies and specialists training.	
"	28		All companies and specialists training.	
"	29		All companies and specialists training.	

T2134. Wt. W708—776. 500000. 4/15. Sir J. C. & S.

Instructions regarding War Diaries and Intelligence Summaries are contained in F. S. Regs., Part II. and the Staff Manual respectively. Title pages will be prepared in manuscript.

WAR DIARY

or

~~INTELLIGENCE SUMMARY~~.

(*Erase heading not required.*) 2/6th BATTN GLOUCESTERSHIRE REGIMENT.

Army Form C. 2118.

Place	Date	Hour	Summary of Events and Information	Remarks and references to Appendices
	1917 JUNE			
OEUF	30		Day of rest. Brigade horse show.	

[illegible] Lieut Col.
Commanding
2/6th Battn Glouc Regt

T2134. Wt. W708—776. 500000. 4/15. Sir J. C. & S.

CONFIDENTIAL

Vol 15

WAR DIARY

of the

2/6th BATTALION THE GLOUCESTERSHIRE REGIMENT

1.7.17 to 31.7.17

(VOLUME 3)

Instructions regarding War Diaries and Intelligence Summaries are contained in F. S. Regs., Part II. and the Staff Manual respectively. Title pages will be prepared in manuscript.

WAR DIARY
or
~~INTELLIGENCE SUMMARY~~.
(Erase heading not required.) 2/6th BATTN GLOUCESTERSHIRE REGIMENT

Army Form C. 2118.

Place	Date	Hour	Summary of Events and Information	Remarks and references to Appendices
	1917 JULY			
OEUF	1		G.O.C. Division presents parchments & ribbons to Brigade.	
"	2		Battalion attack training.	
"	3		All companies training.	
"	4		All companies training.	
"	5		Battalion attack training	
"	6		All companies and specialists training.	
"	7		All companies training.	
"	8		Battalion church parade.	
"	9		All companies and specialists training.	
"	10		Battalion attack practice.	
"	11		All companies and specialists training	
"	12		All companies and specialists training.	
"	13		Battalion attack practice.	
"	14		All companies and specialists training	
"	15		Battalion church parade	
"	16		All companies and specialists training.	

WAR DIARY
or
~~INTELLIGENCE SUMMARY.~~

Army Form C. 2118.

Instructions regarding War Diaries and Intelligence Summaries are contained in F. S. Regs., Part II. and the Staff Manual respectively. Title pages will be prepared in manuscript.

(*Erase heading not required.*) 2/6th BATTN GLOUCESTERSHIRE REGIMENT.

Place	Date	Hour	Summary of Events and Information	Remarks and references to Appendices
	1917 JULY			
OEUF	17		All companies and specialists training	
"	18		All companies training. Divisional race meeting in afternoon	
"	19		All companies and specialists training.	
"	20		Battalion attack practice	
"	21		All companies and specialists training.	
"	22		Battalion church parade	
"	23		Day devoted to Battalion inspection, company training, and interior economy	
"	24		Day devoted to company training and inspection.	
"	25		Battalion moved to PEENHOFF. Marched to PETIT HOUVAIN, where Battalion entrained. Detrained at ESQUELBECQ, & marched to PEENHOFF.	
PEENHOFF	26		Day devoted to interior economy and cleaning	
"	27		All companies training during morning	
"	28		All companies and specialists training during morning.	
"	29		Battalion church parade at night. Day devoted to rest.	

T2134. Wt. W708—776. 500000. 4/15. Sir J. C. & S.

Army Form C. 2118.

WAR DIARY

or

~~INTELLIGENCE SUMMARY.~~

(*Erase heading not required.*) 2/6th BATTN GLOUCESTERSHIRE REGIMENT.

Instructions regarding War Diaries and Intelligence Summaries are contained in F. S. Regs., Part II. and the Staff Manual respectively. Title pages will be prepared in manuscript.

Place	Date	Hour	Summary of Events and Information	Remarks and references to Appendices
	1917 JULY			
PEENHOFF	30		All companies and specialists training	
-	31		All companies and specialists training.	

E. L. Slade Lieut Col.
Commanding 2/6th Battn Glouc Regt

T2134. Wt. W708—776. 500000. 4/15. Sir J. C. & S.

11.16

CONFIDENTIAL

183/61

Vol 16

WAR DIARY

of the

2/6th Battn THE GLOUCESTERSHIRE REGIMENT

from 1.8.17 to 31.8.17

(VOLUME III)

Army Form C. 2118.

Instructions regarding War Diaries and Intelligence Summaries are contained in F. S. Regs., Part II. and the Staff Manual respectively. Title pages will be prepared in manuscript.

WAR DIARY
or
~~INTELLIGENCE SUMMARY.~~

(Erase heading not required.) 2/6th Battn GLOUCESTERSHIRE REGIMENT

Place	Date 1917	Hour	Summary of Events and Information	Remarks and references to Appendices
	August			
PEENHOFF	1		Training.	
Nr ZEGGARS CAPPEL	2		Training	
"	3		Training.	
"	4		Training.	
"	5		Training.	
"	6		Training	
"	7		Training.	
"	8		Training.	
"	9		Training	
"	10		Training	
"	11		Training.	
"	12		Training.	
"	13		Training	
"	14		Training	
"	15		Battn dismounted personell moved by train to POPERINGHE, mounted personell moved by road to POPERINGHE. Entraining station ESQUELBEC. Detraining station HOPOUTRE	(Nr POPERINGHE

T2134. Wt. W708–776. 500000. 4/15. Sir J. C. & S.

WAR DIARY

~~or~~

~~INTELLIGENCE SUMMARY.~~ 2/6 BATT^N GLOUC REG^T

(Erase heading not required.)

Army Form C. 2118.

Instructions regarding War Diaries and Intelligence Summaries are contained in F. S. Regs., Part II. and the Staff Manual respectively. Title pages will be prepared in manuscript.

Place	Date 1917	Hour	Summary of Events and Information	Remarks and references to Appendices
	August			
POPERINGHE	16		Battn moved to Camp in GOLDFISH CHATEAU area near YPRES	
YPRES	17		Battn relieved 15th R.I.R. (36 Division) in Left support at WIELTJE	
WIELTJE	18		Quiet day. Intermittent shelling by night.	
"	19		Quiet day. Intermittent shelling by night.	
"	20		Battn relieved by 4th Ox + BUCKS L.I + moved back to GOLDFISH CHATEAU area (under canvas)	
YPRES	21		Battn moved up to WIELTJE in reserve to 184 Brigade	
WIELTJE TRENCHES	22		184 Brigade attacked. 6 Glos Battn in reserve carrying parties provided	
"	23		Two coys called up for support. A Coy attack [illegible]	
	24		Batt relieved 2/4 Ox + BUCKS L.I. in left sub-sector front line by [illegible]	
	25		Enemy quiet during day except intermittent shelling. Our trenches + positions heavily shelled for two hours starting 11 pm	
	26		Quiet day. Intermittent shelling. [illegible] Batt remaining in position [illegible]	
	27		Artillery [illegible] considerably [illegible] 4th Glouc attacked. Artillery [illegible]	

T2134. Wt. W708—776. 500000. 4/15. Sir J. C. & S.

Instructions regarding War Diaries and Intelligence Summaries are contained in F. S. Regs., Part II. and the Staff Manual respectively. Title pages will be prepared in manuscript.

Army Form C. 2118.

WAR DIARY

~~or~~

~~INTELLIGENCE SUMMARY,~~

(*Erase heading not required.*) 2/6th BATTN. GLOUC REGT.

Place	Date	Hour	Summary of Events and Information	Remarks and references to Appendices
TRENCHES			Battn relieved 2/4th GLOUC in left sector, front line.	
"	28		Artillery quieter on both sides all day.	
"	29		Enemy bombarded our trenches, & positions heavily for an hour at 5AM. Rest of day quiet. Relieved by 2/4 GLOUC, & became Battn in left support.	
"	30		Quiet day. Relieved by 2/7 WARWICKS & moved back to camp, near VLAMERTINGHE.	
VLAMERTINGHE	31		Day devoted to cleaning, baths, & rest.	
			1.8.17	
			[illegible] Lt Col Commanding 2/6 Batt GLOUC REGT.	

T2134. Wt. W708–776. 500000. 4/15. Sir J. C. & S.

2/6 Bn Gloucestershire Regt Vol 17

CONFIDENTIAL.

WAR DIARY.

Sept 1st 1917 – Sept 30th 1917

Instructions regarding War Diaries and Intelligence Summaries are contained in F. S. Regs., Part II. and the Staff Manual respectively. Title pages will be prepared in manuscript.

WAR DIARY

or

~~INTELLIGENCE SUMMARY~~.

(Erase heading not required.) 2/6th Battn GLOUCESTERSHIRE REGIMENT.

Army Form C. 2118

Place	Date	Hour	Summary of Events and Information	Remarks and references to Appendices
	1917 Sept			
VLAMERTINGHE	1		Training	
"	2		Training	
"	3		Training	
"	4		Training	
"	5		Training	
"	6		Training	
"	7		Training.	
"	8		Moved forward to YPRES NORTH area in the evening.	
YPRES N.	9		Interior Economy and Training.	
"	10		Practise attack	
"	11/12		Practise attack Reld 2/7 Worcester Regt in Front line, EAST of WIELTJE.	
In line E of WIELTJE	12		Heavy shelling by boths sides at intervals during the day and night	
"	13		Heavy shelling at intervals Small attack made by the enemy on HINDU COTT, which was easily repulsed by Lewis gun fire.	
"	14		Very quiet day	
"	14/15		Reld by 1/10 Liverpool Regt and moved back to Camp at VLAMERTINGE.	

T2134. Wt. W708—776. 500000. 4/15. Sir J. C. & S.

Instructions regarding War Diaries and Intelligence Summaries are contained in F. S. Regs., Part II. and the Staff Manual respectively. Title pages will be prepared in manuscript.

Army Form C. 2118.

WAR DIARY II

or

~~INTELLIGENCE SUMMARY.~~

(Erase heading not required.) 2/6 BATTN GLOUCESTERSHIRE REGT.

Place	Date	Hour	Summary of Events and Information	Remarks and references to Appendices
VLAMERTINGHE	15.		Moved by 'bus to camp in WATOU No 3 area.	
WATOU AREA	16		Rest.	
"	17		Marched to billets in WORMHOUDT area.	
WORMHOUDT area.	18/19		Marched to CASSEL station, entrained for ARRAS, and marched to billets in SIMENCOURT	
SIMENCOURT	19		Rest.	
"	20		Training	
"	21		Training	
"	22		Training	
"	23		Marched to HULL CAMP, at St NICHOLAS, near ARRAS	
St NICHOLAS	24/25		Relieved 6th DORSET Regt (17 Div) in Left Support. GREENLAND HILL	
Support Trenches	25		Very quiet day. All available men working under R.E.S	
"	26		- do - - do -	
"	27		- do - - do -	
"	28		- do - - do -	
"	29		- do - - do -	

Instructions regarding War Diaries and Intelligence Summaries are contained in F. S. Regs., Part II. and the Staff Manual respectively. Title pages will be prepared in manuscript.

WAR III DIARY

~~or~~

~~INTELLIGENCE SUMMARY.~~

(*Erase heading not required.*)

2/6 GLOUCESTERSHIRE Regt.

Army Form C. 2118.

Place	Date	Hour	Summary of Events and Information	Remarks and references to Appendices
SUPPORT TRENCH	30		Very quiet day. Relieved 2/4 Glos Regt in the evening. in the left sub-section in the line. without incident.	

W. L. [illegible] Major.
Commanding 2/6 Glos Regt.

T2134. Wt. W708—776. 500000. 4/15. Sir J. C. & S.

2/6 Gloucester Regt
Vol 18

CONFIDENTIAL

WAR DIARY

Oct 1 - 31 - 1917.

Instructions regarding War Diaries and Intelligence Summaries are contained in F. S. Regs., Part II. and the Staff Manual respectively. Title pages will be prepared in manuscript.

WAR DIARY
or
~~INTELLIGENCE SUMMARY.~~

(*Erase heading not required.*) 2/6 GLOUCESTERSHIRE REGT.

Army Form C. 2118.

Place	Date	Hour	Summary of Events and Information	Remarks and references to Appendices
	October			
TRENCHES.	1		In front line GREENLAND HILL SECTOR very quiet day.	
-	2		-do- -do- -do-	
-	3		-do- -do- -do-	
-	4		-do- -do- -do- Relieved by 2/1 Bucks Regt and moved back to HULL CAMP, St NICHOLAS, N ARRAS, becoming a Battn. in Divsl reserve.	
St NICHOLAS (NR ARRAS)	5		Baths and Cleaning up	
	6		Training	
-	7		Church Parade	
-	8		Training	
-	9		-do-	
-	10		-do-	
-	11		-do-	
-	12		-do-	
-	13		-do-	
-	14		Church Parade	

T2134. Wt. W708—776. 500000. 4/15. Sir J. C. & S.

OCTOBER.

Instructions regarding War Diaries and Intelligence Summaries are contained in F. S. Regs., Part II. and the Staff Manual respectively. Title pages will be prepared in manuscript.

WAR DIARY

~~or~~

~~INTELLIGENCE SUMMARY.~~

(Erase heading not required.) 2/6th GLOUCESTERSHIRE REGT.

Army Form C. 2118.

Place	Date	Hour	Summary of Events and Information	Remarks and references to Appendices
	October			
St NICHOLAS (NR ARRAS)	15		Training.	
"	16		Relieved 2/8th WARWICK REGT in CHEMICAL WORKS Sector, left support.	
SUPPORT TRENCHES	17		Working parties	
–	18		– do –	
–	19		– do –	
–	20		– do –	
–	21		– do –	
–	22		Reld 2/4 GLOS Regt in FRONT LINE, without incident.	
FRONT LINE TRENCHES	23		Quiet day. Some retaliation in evening as a result of a raid made by Battn on our left. 1 O.R. Killed 2 O.R. Wounded.	
"	24		2/4 Glos Regt & 2/7 Worcester Regt raided the enemy trenches on our front in the afternoon. Heavy retaliation by enemy artillery, doing considerable damage to trenches. Enemy again retaliated on our front during and after a raid made by a Battn on our left in the evening. 1 O.R killed and 7 O.R wounded as a result of this.	
–	25		Quiet day.	

T2134. Wt W708—776. 500000. 4/15. Sir J. C. & S.

Instructions regarding War Diaries and Intelligence Summaries are contained in F. S. Regs., Part II. and the Staff Manual respectively. Title pages will be prepared in manuscript.

OCTOBER 1917 **WAR DIARY** ~~or INTELLIGENCE SUMMARY.~~

Army Form C. 2118.

(*Erase heading not required.*) 2/6 GLOUCESTERSHIRE REGT.

Place	Date	Hour	Summary of Events and Information	Remarks and references to Appendices
	October/17			
FRONT LINE TRENCHES	26		Quiet day. very little shelling	
"	27		very quiet day	
"	28		- do - 2/4 GLOS REGT reld us in the evening, this Battn moving back to support trenches.	
SUPPORT TRENCHES	29		Working Parties. In the evening a party picked from 'A' Coy of 3 Officers (including O.C. Coy) & 60 O.R. raided the enemys trenches. No prisoners were brought back or war material. but 2 enemy sentries were killed, one deep dug out containing Germans was bombed, and a M.G. firing on the parapet was put out of action. Our casualties were:- One Officer wounded and missing, 2 O.R. missing. 14 O.R. wounded.	
"	30		working parties	
"	31		- do -	

E B Slade

Lieut Col:

Commdg 2/6th GLOS Regt.

T2134. Wt. W708—776. 500000. 4/15. Sir J. C. & S.

2/6th Bn The Gloucestershire Regt

CONFIDENTIAL

WAR DIARY

NOVEMER 1 - 30 1917

Instructions regarding War Diaries and Intelligence Summaries are contained in F. S. Regs., Part II. and the Staff Manual respectively. Title pages will be prepared in manuscript.

WAR DIARY
or
~~INTELLIGENCE SUMMARY~~.
(Erase heading not required.)

2/6 Gloster Regt.

Army Form C. 2118.

Place	Date	Hour	Summary of Events and Information	Remarks and references to Appendices
	1917 Nov			
In Trenches	1		CHEMICAL WORKS Sector – working parties	
"	2		Nothing to report	
"	3		Relieved 2/4 GLOSTER REGT in line	
"	4		Enemy Artillery very active in reply to daylight raid by 47 DIVISION on LEFT	
"	5		Quiet day. Enemy Artillery fairly lively during hours of darkness	
"	6		Quiet day. Enemy twice attempted to get through our wire during hours	
"			of darkness but failed.	
"	7		Quiet day	
"	8		Quiet	
"	9		Relieved by 2/1 BUCKS Bn and moved back to ARRAS. Billetted at Prison.	
ARRAS	10		Battalion to Baths.	
"	11		Church Parade – Draft of 36 reported from Depot Battalion	
"	12		Working parties and fatigues.	
"	13.		Training – In afternoon Football match v 2/4 GLOSTERS – Conference at Brigade	
"			H.Q. in evening.	
"	14		Training. In afternoon all officers + NCOs to musketry Lecture by Major SOMERVILLE DSO	

T2134. Wt. W708—776. 500000. 4/15. Sir J. C. & S.

Instructions regarding War Diaries and Intelligence Summaries are contained in F. S. Regs., Part II. and the Staff Manual respectively. Title pages will be prepared in manuscript.

WAR DIARY
or
~~INTELLIGENCE SUMMARY.~~ 2/6 GLOSTER REGT.

(Erase heading not required.)

Army Form C. 2118.

Place	Date	Hour	Summary of Events and Information	Remarks and references to Appendices
	1917			
ARRAS	Nov 15		Training - Musketry on Range - Battalion Boxing Competition - Working parties & fatigues	
"	16		Brigade Musketry Competition	
"	17		Brigade Musketry Competition	
"	18		Church Parade	
"	19		Brigade Order No 157 received to move up into LEFT Support GREENLAND HILL Sector and take over from 2/6 ROYAL WARWICK REGT on 21st. Commanding Officer to line	
"	20		Nothing to report	
"	21		Relieved 2/6 ROYAL WARWICK REGT in LEFT Support. Relief complete by 4.25 pm Lt Col E.C. SLADE D.S.O. M.C. went to Hospital sick and Capt C.R. ALLEN assumed command	
In Trenches	22		Quiet day. Dull. Working on trenches.	
"	23		Work on trenches. Carrying parties at night.	
"	24		ditto ditto	
"	25		ditto ditto	
"	26		Brigade Order No 160 received to take over Front line LEFT subsection on night 27/28	
"	27		Relief commenced when orders were received from Brigade that B.O. 160 was cancelled and instructions were received to return to previous positions. Orders received that Bn would be relieved by 6 Cameron Highlanders tomorrow.	
"	28		Relieved by 2 Companies 6 Cameron Highlanders. Withdrew to billets in ARRAS.	

T2131. Wt. W708—776. 500000. 4/15. Sir J. C. & S.

Instructions regarding War Diaries and Intelligence Summaries are contained in F. S. Regs., Part II. and the Staff Manual respectively. Title pages will be prepared in manuscript.

WAR DIARY
or
~~INTELLIGENCE~~ SUMMARY.
(Erase heading not required.)

Army Form C. 2118.

2/6 Gloster Regt.

Place	Date	Hour	Summary of Events and Information	Remarks and references to Appendices
	1917 Nov			
ARRAS	29		Battn prepared for move. Baths and cleaning up.	
ARRAS	30		Battn moved to BARASTRE S.E. of BAPAUME. Mounted personell by road, dismounted personell by train from ~~[illegible]~~ DAINVILLE station to BAPAUME, & then by road to BARASTRE.	

W. C. Ruthven.
Major
Comdg 2/6 Glos Regt.

T2134. Wt. W708—776. 500000. 4/15. Sir J. C. & S.

CONFIDENTIAL

WAR DIARY

of.

2/6 GLOUCESTERSHIRE REGT.

from December 1st 1917 to December 31st 1917

Instructions regarding War Diaries and Intelligence Summaries are contained in F. S. Regs., Part II. and the Staff Manual respectively. Title pages will be prepared in manuscript.

WAR DIARY
or
~~INTELLIGENCE SUMMARY~~.
(Erase heading not required.)

Army Form C. 2118.

2/6 GLOUCESTERSHIRE Regt.

Place	Date	Hour	Summary of Events and Information	Remarks and references to Appendices
December		1917		
METZ	1		Battn bivouacked in HAYRINCOURT WOOD. Moved up to the line in the afternoon and took over the line E of LAVACQUERIE, in and about the HINDENBURG LINE.	
TRENCHES E. of LA VACQUERIE	2		Enemy made an attack on one of our saps (part of HINDENBURG LINE) about 6am with a large party. He drove us back twice, but local counter attacks re-captured the ground. about 6.30 am. the enemy attacked again with a larger party gained and held the sap, owing to ~~the~~ our supply of bombs having run out. about 2pm. after a heavy barrage, the enemy attacked with large forces on a fairly wide front bombing down trenches and attacking across the open. We were forced to retire about 300 yards. Counter attacks were made to drive the enemy back, but without success. Battn H.Q. was captured during this attack, the Commanding Officer being hit near B H.Q. & believed to have been taken prisoner. At night several attacks were made on our new positions, but all were repulsed.	
"	3		At dawn, the enemy continued his attack (under an intense bombardment), up trenches and over the open. The main attack was made on our right flank, but small bombing attacks were made on the ground held, by ~~[illegible]~~	

Instructions regarding War Diaries and Intelligence Summaries are contained in F. S. Regs., Part II. and the Staff Manual respectively. Title pages will be prepared in manuscript.

WAR DIARY ~~or~~ ~~INTELLIGENCE~~ SUMMARY.

(*Erase heading not required.*)

Army Form C. 2118.

II 2/6 GLOUCESTERSHIRE REGT

Place	Date	Hour	Summary of Events and Information	Remarks and references to Appendices
	December	1917		
			the remaining Officers and men of the Battn. which at times were partially successful, but finally the enemy was driven back to his original position. The attack ~~on~~ our right flank was successful, the enemy finally occupying the village of LA VACQUERIE.	
TRENCHES E of LA VACQUERIE	4		In the early morning the remaining part of the Battn withdrew ~~to [illegible]~~ ~~to [illegible]~~, owing to the fact that, with the enemy occupying the village, it would have been impossible to hold on in their position. Fairly quiet day. no attack was made. Battn was attached to the 2/4 GLOS Regt.	
TRENCHES E of VILLERS PLOUICH	5		Fairly quiet day. In the evening we were relieved by 2/1 BUCKS and became Battn in Brigade reserve. Later we were relieved by 2/5 GLOS Regt and moved back to bivouacs in HAVRINCOURT WOOD.	
			Casualties for Dec 2nd/5th estimated as follows:- 2 Officers and 18 O.R. Killed 12 " and 140 O.R. Wounded 3 " and 150 O.R. Missing	
HAVRINCOURT WOOD	6		Battn on working party, digging new Reserve line.	
"	7		" " " " from 6.30 am till 12.30 pm. Re-organisation of the	

Army Form C. 2118.

Instructions regarding War Diaries and Intelligence Summaries are contained in F. S. Regs., Part II. and the Staff Manual respectively. Title pages will be prepared in manuscript.

WAR DIARY
or
~~INTELLIGENCE SUMMARY.~~

(Erase heading not required.)

III

2/6 GLOUCESTERSHIRE Regt

Place	Date	Hour	Summary of Events and Information	Remarks and references to Appendices
December		1917		
			Baths in the afternoon. Formed 2 Coys of 2 platoons per Company.	
HAVRINCOURT WOOD	8		100 O.R. on working party from 4.30 am till 10.30 am. Inspection by G.O.C Brigade in the afternoon.	
–	9		Inspection by G.O.C Division in the morning. After the Inspection Coys carried out training and re-organising. The camp and area was shelled at intervals during the day, but no damage was done. Eighty men bathed at METZ in afternoon.	
–	10		~~Baths~~ Preparations made for moving into the line. Relieved 2/1 BUCKS in the line E of VILLERS PLUICH.	
TRENCHES. E of VILLERS PLUICH	11		Very quiet day.	
–	12		Quiet day. Only occassional shelling. A message was received late in the evening that it seemed likely that the enemy would be attacking at 6.30 am on the 13th. Special precautions were made in view of this message.	
–	13		Owing to the likelihood of an enemy attack, our artillery and machine guns opened fairly heavily at 5.30 am and continued till 7.10 am, firing on S.O.S lines and all likely places where enemy would be	

T2134. Wt. W708–776. 500000. 4/15. Sir J. C. & S.

Instructions regarding War Diaries and Intelligence Summaries are contained in F. S. Regs., Part II. and the Staff Manual respectively. Title pages will be prepared in manuscript.

WAR DIARY ~~or~~ ~~INTELLIGENCE~~ SUMMARY. IV

(*Erase heading not required.*)

Army Form C. 2118.

2/6 GLOUCESTERSHIRE Regt

Place	Date	Hour	Summary of Events and Information	Remarks and references to Appendices
December 1917				
			forming up, also on LA VACQUERIE. No attack was made by the enemy and very little retaliation.	
			Again, at 12 noon till 12.30 pm, our guns were very active. The enemy retaliated on our front and support lines with 5.9's & 4.2's, doing very little damage. All quiet by 12.45 pm.	
TRENCHES E of VILLERS PLOUICH	14		Quiet day. Relieved by 2/4 GLOS Regt in evening and moved back to reserve trenches on BEAUCHAMP RIDGE and became Battn in Brigade reserve.	
TRENCHES (RESERVE) BEAUCHAMP RIDGE	15		Lightly shelled in the morning, causing five casualties. 2 O.R. killed and 3 O.R. wounded. Work on shelters and trenches during day. Carrying party of 60 O.R. provided at night for carrying R.E. material.	
–	16		Quiet day. Work on shelters and trenches; also carrying parties.	
–	17		– – – – – – – – – –	
–	18		– – – – – – – – – –	
–	19		– – – – – – – – – –	
–	20		– – – – – – – – – –	
–	21		– – – – – – – – – –	

T2134. Wt. W708–776. 500000. 4/15. Sir J. C. & S.

Instructions regarding War Diaries and Intelligence Summaries are contained in F. S. Regs., Part II. and the Staff Manual respectively. Title pages will be prepared in manuscript.

Army Form C. 2118.

WAR DIARY ~~or~~ ~~INTELLIGENCE SUMMARY~~. V

2/6 GLOUCESTERSHIRE Regt

(*Erase heading not required.*)

Place	Date	Hour	Summary of Events and Information	Remarks and references to Appendices
December 1917				
RESERVE TRENCHES BEAUCAMP RIDGE	22		Quiet day. Working parties. Reld in the early evening by 2 Coys HOWE Bn R.N. Division and moved back to camp in HAVRINCOURT WOOD.	
HAVRINCOURT WOOD.	23		Moved to camp at ETRICOURT.	
ETRICOURT	24		Battn. less transport, entrained at ETRICOURT station and de-trained at PLATEAU. BRAY sur SOMME. and marched to CHIPILLY. Transport proceeded to CHIPILLY by road, arriving at 11.30 pm	
CHIPILLY	25		Church parade in morning. Remainder of day spent in cleaning billets.	
"	26		General inspections and interior economy. Re-organised Battn into 2 Companies of 3 platoons per Coy.	
"	27		Training.	
"	28		Baths at MORCOURT in morning. Training in the afternoon. Inspection of Transport in the afternoon by G.O.C. Brigade.	
"	29		Draft of two Officers and 67 OR reported from Div Depot Bn – Reorganised Bn into 4 Companies of 2 Platoons each.	
"	30		Bde Operation order No 174 received. for move to WIENCOURT by road tomorrow. Church Parade.	

T2134. Wt. W708–776. 500000. 4/15. Sir J. C. & S.

Instructions regarding War Diaries and Intelligence Summaries are contained in F. S. Regs., Part II. and the Staff Manual respectively. Title pages will be prepared in manuscript.

WAR DIARY

or

~~INTELLIGENCE SUMMARY~~.

(Erase heading not required.)

2/6 GLOUCESTERSHIRE Reg[illegible]

Place	Date	Hour	Summary of Events and Information	Remarks and references to Appendices
December 1917				
CHIPILLY	31		Moved to WIENCOURT by road and billetted there. Transport proceeded by longer route on account of bad state of roads.	

J M Foster
Lt Col
Comdg 2/6 Glosters.

T2134. Wt. W708—776. 500000. 4/15. Sir J. C. & S.

Vol 21

January 1918

War Diary

~ of ~

2/6th Battn The Gloucester Regt

Instructions regarding War Diaries and Intelligence Summaries are contained in F. S. Regs., Part II. and the Staff Manual respectively. Title pages will be prepared in manuscript.

WAR DIARY
or
~~INTELLIGENCE SUMMARY~~.
(Erase heading not required.)

2/6 GLOSTERSHIRE REGT.

Army Form C. 2118.

Place	Date	Hour	Summary of Events and Information	Remarks and references to Appendices
	1918			
WIENCOURT	JAN 1		Battalion muster parade. Coy Training –	
"	2		Training	
"	3		Training	
"	4		Training	
"	5		Training	
"	6		Church Parades. Platoon demonstration after Church parade	
"	7		Battn moved by road, to ROIGLISE near ROYE	
ROIGLISE	8		Clearing up and general inspection.	
"	9		Battn moved by road to FALVY	
FALVY	10		Training.	
"	11		Training working party on clearing roads.	
"	12		Training	
"	13		Church Parade. Working Party on clearing roads.	
"	14		Training	
"	15		Battn moved to UGNY by road.	
UGNY	16		Training. Baths	

T2134. Wt. W708–776. 500000. 4/15. Sir J. C. & S.

Instructions regarding War Diaries and Intelligence Summaries are contained in F. S. Regs., Part II. and the Staff Manual respectively. Title pages will be prepared in manuscript.

Army Form C. 2118.

WAR DIARY
or
INTELLIGENCE SUMMARY.
(Erase heading not required.)

Place	Date	Hour	Summary of Events and Information	Remarks and references to Appendices
UGNY	17		Training. Reconnaissance of new line	
"	18		Cleaning up for trenches. Reconnaissance of new line.	
"	19		Battn relieved 2/5 R. WARWICKS in left sub sector of right sector.	
TRENCHES E of FAYET and N.W. of ST QUENTIN	20		Very quiet day	
	21		- do -	
"	22		- do - Battn relieved by 2/4 GLOS Regt and moved back to quarters in HOLNON WOOD. becoming LEFT SUPPORT BATTN.	
HOLNON WOOD	23		Battn on working parties	
"	24		- do -	
"	25		- do -	
"	26		- do - Relieved 2/4 Glos Regt in left sub sector of right sector	
TRENCHES	27		Quiet day	
"	28		- do -	
"	29		- do -	
"	30		- do - Relvd by 2/4 GLOS Regt and moved back to quarters in HOLNON WOOD	
HOLNON WOOD	31		BATTN on WORKING PARTIES	

T2134. Wt. W708–776. 500000. 4/15. Sir J. C. & S.

[signature] Lieut Col Comdg 2/6 GLOS Regt.

40

H.Qrs
61st Div. Q

Herewith completed War Diary for 2/6th Bn Gloster R up to the day of disbandment

Gardner Capt for ......Lieut, Col.

Commanding 2/6th. B'n. Gloster Regt.

20/2/18

2/6TH BATTALION,
GLOSTER REGIMENT.
No. 3216 Q
Date 21.2.18.

Army Form C. 2118.

Instructions regarding War Diaries and Intelligence Summaries are contained in F. S. Regs., Part II. and the Staff Manual respectively. Title pages will be prepared in manuscript.

WAR DIARY
or
~~INTELLIGENCE~~ SUMMARY.
(Erase heading not required.)

2/6 Bn GLOUCESTER REGT.

VR 22

Place	Date	Hour	Summary of Events and Information	Remarks and references to Appendices
February 1918				
HOLNON WOOD	1		Battn on working parties	
	2		-do-	
–	3		-do- Relieved in evening by 2/5th GLOS Regt and moved back to VAUX, becoming a Battn of the Brigade in Divisional Reserve.	
VAUX	4		Battn on working parties. ~~and bath~~	
–	5		– – – – and Bathing	
–	6		– – – – . Inspection of Battn in afternoon by G.O.C Brigade This is the last time that Battn paraded as a Battn, being disbanded and drafts sent to various units.	
–	7		150 O.R proceeded to MARTEVILLE, and joined 2/5 GLOS Regt. The remainder of the Battn, less Transport & Q.M. Stores, moved to GUIZANCOURT & QUIVIERES.	
GUIZANCOURT			Transport complete. 1 Officer & 35 O.R. proceeded by road to join 57th Division Q.M. Stores moved to QUIVIERES. Battalion training.	
–	9		Training.	
–	10		Training. & Church parade.	
–	11		Training. 8 Officers proceeded to MARTEVILLE, and joined 2/5th Glos Regt.	

T2134. Wt. W708—776. 500000. 4/15. Sir J. C. & S.

Instructions regarding War Diaries and Intelligence Summaries are contained in F. S. Regs., Part II. and the Staff Manual respectively. Title pages will be prepared in manuscript.

WAR DIARY

~~or~~ II

~~INTELLIGENCE SUMMARY.~~

(Erase heading not required.)

2/6 Bn GLOUCESTERSHIRE REGT.

Army Form C. 2118.

Place	Date	Hour	Summary of Events and Information	Remarks and references to Appendices
	February 1918			
GUIZANCOURT	12		working parties all day on aerodrome	
"	13		- do -	
"	14		- do -	
"	15		- do -	
"	16		- do -	
"	17		- do -	
"	18		- do -	
"	19		- do -	
	20.		Lieut. Col. F. W. Foster remained in Div. Area. R.S.M. (Hospital) R.Q.M.S. + 2. C.Q.M.S. transferred to "D." I.B.D. All remaining officers W.O.s N.C.Os + men of the Battn. transferred to 24th Entrenching Battn and moved to LANGUEVOISIN where they came under orders of Lieut. Col. D. G. Barnsley O.C. 24th Entrenching Battn	
			2/6th Battn Gloucester Regt. does not now exist.	
			20/2/18. [signature] Gardner Capt Comdg 2/6 Glost Regt.	

T2134. Wt. W708-[illegible] 25. Sir [illegible] 8.

2/7 Bn Worcs Reg.

SEP 1915 — JAN 1918

www.ingramcontent.com/pod-product-compliance
Lightning Source LLC
Chambersburg PA
CBHW081356160426
43192CB00013B/2425
9781474533201